MARKET GUIDE

FOR

Young Artists
and
Photographers

Other Books by Kathy Henderson:

Market Guide for Young Writers
What Would We Do Without You? A Guide to
  Volunteer Activities for Kids
I Can Be a . . .
  Farmer
  Horse Trainer
  Rancher
  Basketball Player
New True Books
  Dairy Cows
  Great Lakes
  Christmas Trees

MARKET GUIDE
FOR
Young Artists
and
Photographers

KATHY HENDERSON

SHOE TREE PRESS
WHITE HALL, VIRGINIA

Published by Shoe Tree Press, an imprint of
Betterway Publications, Inc.
P.O. Box 219
Crozet, VA 22932
(804) 823-5661

Cover design by Susan Riley
Typography by Park Lane Associates

Library of Congress Cataloging-in-Publication Data

Henderson, Kathy
    Market guide for young artists and photographers / by Kathy
Henderson.
    p.   cm.
    Includes index.
    Summary: Lists over 100 markets and contests open to artists and
photographers eighteen and under, offers marketing tips and
guidelines, and profiles successful young artists.
    ISBN 1-55870-176-1 : $10.95
    1. Art--United States--Marketing--Juvenile literature.
2. Photography--United States--Marketing--Juvenile literature.
[1. Art--Marketing. 2. Photography--Marketing.] I. Title.
N8600.H46 1990
706'.8'8--dc20   90-39084
                                               CIP
                                             AC

Printed in the United States of America
0 9 8 7 6 5 4 3 2 1

*For my son Eric, who
has always brought an extra measure of joy
to my life through his art.*

Acknowledgments

The author and publisher of this *Guide* deeply appreciate the generous cooperation of editors, contest sponsors, and fellow writers who have contributed information and ideas for this edition.

With special thanks to:

Ashley Callen
Kathryn Jessica Hull
Emily Davidson
Marisa Fiordalisi
Paul Haidle
Elizabeth Haidle
Amity Gaige
Janelle Colby
Kevin Berlin

William Rubel
David Melton
Deborah Valentine
Tracey Holloway
Ellen S. Thomas
Richard M. Myers
Mercedes A. Quiroga
Larry W. Wood
Mike Wilmer

Contents

Foreword

By Trina Schart Hyman [excerpt from
Self-Portrait: Trina Schart Hyman, by Trina
Schart Hyman, 1981, Addison-Wesley.]

"I was a really strange little kid. I was born terrified of anything and everything that moved or spoke. I was afraid of people, especially. All people − kids my own age, all grownups, even my own family. Dogs (until my parents bought me a puppy of my own), horses, trees, grass, cars, streets. I was afraid of the stars and the wind. Who knows why?

"My mother is a beautiful woman with red hair and the piercing blue gaze of a hawk. She never seemed afraid of anyone or anything. It was she who gave me the courage to draw and a love of books. She read to me from the time I was a baby, and once, when I was three or four and she was reading my favorite story, the words on the page, her spoken words, and the scenes in my head fell together in a blinding flash. I could read!

"When I had to have braces on my teeth, for nine years, my father drove me into the city to the orthodonist every Saturday morning. I'm sure he would much rather have spent the time fishing the quiet backwaters he loved, but for me, those city trips were journeys into a magical kingdom. Some Saturdays, after the dentist, I got to go to the Philadelphia Art Museum as a reward.

"I should have been afraid of that grand, imposing building, but I wasn't. I loved it. I loved the vales and glades and corridors full of paintings, and the tapestries and glass and wood and furniture that the artists who had done the painting must have used or known! Or at least thought about.

"Although I skipped first grade, I was a terrible student. I couldn't ever concentrate on what I was supposed to be learning about, because all I wanted to do was to be left alone, to read books or listen to music, or to draw pictures of witches or princesses when I should have been learning fractions. After eleven years, I came out of the public school system believing I was a hopelessy stupid little creature who would never be able to learn or to think.

"I could draw, though, and after I graduated from high school, I went to art school in Philadelphia, and then everything changed. Suddenly, I was not only *allowed* to draw all day long, I was *expected* to! I was surrounded by other artists all day, and we talked, ate, lived and dreamed about art. It was as though I had been living, all my life, in a strange country where I could never quite fit in — and now I had come home.

"After the first year of basic drawing, painting, printmaking and design classes, I majored in illustration. My best friend, Barbara, was an illustration major, too. Barbara and I went everywhere together; we'd walk all over the city, drawing everything we saw: people, streets, doorways, subways, trees, piles of trash. If we discovered a "new" street, we were as excited as if we'd found a new world. Whenever we had any free time, we'd walk to the art museum and wander through its miles of beautiful rooms and quiet corridors, looking at paintings and drawing from them. And every day for lunch, rain or shine, we went to Rittenhouse Square. We took our sketch books, hamburgers, coffee and a big box of saltines for the crowds of pigeons.

"We were comrades; we were *artists*. Everything was exciting and beautiful, and we loved it all."

Nothing like *Market Guide for Young Artists and Photographers* was available when I was a child. I wish it had been. Then, maybe, I would have realized sooner that not being very good in school *didn't* automatically mean I wasn't a worthwhile person.

Discovering markets and contests where I might share my work would have been challenging, full of excitement and hope. Imagine learning that someone other than the family and friends likes your work enough to display it where hundreds or thousands of people might see it!

I probably would have found it a bit scary, too. And terribly disappointing if my work was returned or didn't win a competition.

But, part of being an artist is having faith in yourself and in your work, and the courage to keep on trying. Just knowing that there were so many opportunities open to a young artist like myself would have been comforting and encouraging.

Today's young artists, photographers, and writers are lucky to have a resource such as this available to them. I hope they'll draw comfort and encouragement from it, as well as take advantage of the many opportunities that exist.

I wish everyone of you success. After all, we are all comrades. We are *artists*.

PREFACE

A Word to Parents and Teachers

There are many traditional opportunities that exist for young artists and photographers to display their creative work — from the front of their family's refrigerator to bulletin boards at school to windows of local stores and restaurants, particularly during holiday seasons. But other opportunities abound in the pages of magazines and books, as well as numerous contests and shows. But, like young writers, few young artists and photographers knew previously where and how to access these alternative markets and contests.

Market Guide for Young Artists & Photographers, like its predecessor *Market Guide for Young Writers*, was written as much with you in mind as the young people with whom you are involved. It is the first of its kind to bring together the wide variety of publications and contests that are especially accessible to young artists and photographers eighteen and under. Over 300 editors, art directors, and contest sponsors were queried in regard to their policies, payments, and the potential for young people to have work accepted. In addition, many editors and contest sponsors offered specific tips to help them get started. The result is a unique collection of many of the best opportunities for young people. Counting not only the listings themselves, but the number of opportunities that exist *within* each listing, nearly 100 opportunities are represented.

Please note, however, that many of the most exciting and accessible opportunities for young artists and photographers still exist within their local, regional, and state communities. In many ways, these "home-town" opportunities for young artists and photographers far outnumber the ones for young writers. Only a sampling of these many and varied types of opportunities, which often have residency restrictions, have been included in this *Guide* because of space limitations. You and your young person can locate such opportunities by watching or listening for notices in local and regional newspapers, magazines, and radio and television programs. Check also with local, regional, and state art councils, or with the art departments at local schools and colleges. While some local art shows and contests have age restrictions, many do not. And those that do may be willing to sponsor special categories for young people if you let them know there is adequate interest.

Since a young person needs to know more than just where to send work, *Market Guide for Young Artists & Photographers* also contains information on preparing work for submission, including some tips for accompanying manuscripts. Yet, the entire Guide, with its special charts and easy-to-follow directions, is easy enough for students as young as nine to use on their own.

You will find it just as useful as a reference guide for artists of any age interested in publishing their work. Something I found especially interesting is the fact that a number of "art" markets and contests are more concerned with the message that the submitter has attempted to convey, rather than whether the finished piece is exceptionally artistic in terms of execution quality. This is good news especially for young people with good ideas but not necessarily a good hand and eye for art.

A special chapter called "Young Artists and Photographers in Print" provides a wealth of insight and inspiration from young people who have already been successful in accessing markets and contests in which to publish or display their work. These students represent a wide range of ages, backgrounds, and interests. A second profile chapter, "Editors Are Real People Too," will give both you and your young artist or photographer a unique behind-the-scenes look into a variety of markets and contests.

It is important to remember that the goal of this *Guide* is not riches and fame for young people even though a number of markets and contests have substantial rewards. Its primary purpose is to provide young artists and photographers the means to reach beyond their circle of friends, family, and teachers, to explore and share their innermost thoughts creatively, to unleash their imaginations, and to realize the excitement and benefits that can be obtained by using their minds and talents to communicate effectively. Like *Market Guide for Young Writers*, *Market Guide for Young Artists & Photographers* is a book that I, and many other people, wish had been available years ago for our own use.

CHAPTER ONE
Getting Started

Today's young artists and photographers, including budding video and film buffs, have more opportunities than ever before to share their creative work with the public. However, before you can take advantage of these opportunities, you need to know *where they are and how* to submit material to them. *Market Guide for Young Artists & Photographers* has that special information, plus a lot more.

The market and contest lists in this book are the results of a special survey of editors and contest sponsors across the United States and Canada. Their enthusiastic response made it possible to group together a promising list of publications and contests for you to try. Many of the magazines listed have specific sections illustrated with artwork and photographs created entirely by young people. Other magazines, such as those whose readers are mainly adults, are willing to consider the work of young people.

A variety of other related market and contest opportunities are also included. Most often, these opportunities are for written material that can be submitted on its own merits or as a complement to your artwork, particularly photos and illustrations. For more complete information about submitting creative written work (called manuscripts) to markets and contests, see the current edition of the *Market Guide for Young Writers*.

Why are so many editors, art directors, and contest sponsors interested in submissions from you? The answer is simple: many of them were once young artists and photographers too! They haven't forgotten, nor lost, the desire to share what they have created with others. They also know how talented young people can be and consider it a privilege to share their work in a positive and professional way.

Many of these markets and contests not only publish material in the pages of their various publications, or otherwise display it to the public, but offer payment, and cash prizes as well. Instead of payment others offer free copies of issues containing your work. Sometimes they offer both. As you search through the lists, pay special attention to entries marked with an asterisk (*). Markets and contests bearing this symbol are especially interested in receiving material from young people. They usually have special columns, departments, or category divisions for young people and therefore will accept more material from young artists than will other markets.

Please note that a number of markets and many contests require an entry or subscription fee. These listings are marked with a dollar sign ($). They have been included because they have special sections for young writers, have been known to use a large amount of material created by young people, or have indicated that they are particularly interested in submissions from young people. These markets and contests should be considered only after careful examination. Make sure your material is good enough to make the payment of an entry or other fee a worthwhile investment.

Consider, too, why an entry fee has been requested and what the collected fees will be used for. Note also that for various reasons, it is much more common for an art contest, especially one that features a display of all or most contest submissions in either a future publication or gallery-type show, to request an entry fee. One reason for this is that it often costs the publisher or contest sponsor more to publish artwork as opposed to written manuscripts. Color photography and illustrations in particular are especially expensive to reproduce. Beware of contests that make everyone who enters a winner, or a market that publishes almost anything submitted, as long as the authors are willing to buy a copy of the contest's anthology.

There are often costs involved when submitting graphic images, messages, and library files to "on-line" markets and contests. Included in these costs are subscription fees and connect charges to access an information service such as CompuServe or GEnie. However, a dollar sign ($) will not appear with these listings unless a separate entry fee or surcharge is also charged to enter a contest or to participate within a special interest group (SIG). In many ways, these connect charges are similar to the normal expenses, such as paper, envelopes, and stamps, involved with submitting to traditional markets. Note that basic connect charges are often waived anytime you upload material to a SIG library.

Give Yourself an Edge

Unfortunately, no one can guarantee that you will find a willing market to publish and/or display your work. However, there are several things to keep in mind when searching for, and submitting to, opportunities; things that will often give your material an edge against the competition.

1. Send only your very best work.

Whether you snap photographs, draw cartoons and comic strips, make documentary or "for fun" videos and film, or write and illustrate your own stories, not *everything* you create will be of publishable quality. Just like a musician or athlete, a lot of what we do is practice, whether we like to admit it or not. Spend time planning your project. You may need to make dozens of preliminary sketches or rewrite and re-shoot a scene before it conveys the message and emotion of what you intended to share. It often helps to ask someone, such as a knowledgeable adult or peer, for their opinion of your finished work before you submit it. You may or may not agree with their comments and want to work further on your project before submitting it. However, just hearing someone else's opinion will often help you to see your material in a new way. Yet always remember that you are the creator. You should be the final judge of whether your work is ready to share.

2. Before submitting a work to a particular market or contest, make sure it is in a format and medium that is acceptable to that market or contest.

While there isn't space here to describe the usual format for *every* type of art medium (paintings, illustrations, video tape, cartoon strips, color slides, black and white glossy prints, etc.), there are some standards to follow. They are included in Chapter Four of this Guide.

In addition, many magazines and contests offer tip sheets for submitting artwork and photography as well as manuscripts. Take the time to send for these, and follow them as closely as possible.

3. Protect your artwork from damage while you are creating it, but especially when you store it or prepare it for submission.

As with manuscripts, the *condition* in which your artwork arrives is as important as what it is meant to show. Wrinkled, torn, and smudged illustrations, or photographs with paper clip marks or furrows made by writing with a lead pencil or ball point pen not only make a poor first impression, they sometimes make it impossible to reproduce the work well enough to meet the high standards of the publication or contest. Consult some of the resources listed in the Appendix to learn the best ways to store your art and photographs. Also invest in an art portfolio case or make your own from heavy cardboard with acetate and/or tissue inserts to help keep your work neat and clean.

4. Study the market and contest information carefully before submitting any type of work.

There are many reasons why editors and art directors will reject material. But by far, the biggest and most aggravating reason for rejection is something editors call *inappropriate submission*. This means that that particular publication or contest never uses the type of material you have submitted. For instance, if a market says it wants pen and ink illustrations, do not send an acrylic watercolor no matter how good a painting you think it is. And don't send a color photo of any size when it says it only accepts black and white glossies, 5" X 7" preferred.

Also make certain your submission is appropriate in theme or subject matter. For example, a magazine that specializes in science fiction and fantasy isn't going to be interested in seeing your illustrations of cute, cuddly, lap animals. And a market that only publishes how-to articles and personal experience essays about writing won't want to see the book about a dinosaur, which you wrote and illustrated in class.

Be sure to take the time to study individual market and contest information carefully. Send for and study the guidelines or tip sheets. Buy, send for, or find a sample issue if you are not familiar with the publication. Then look it over objectively to determine if your photos or artwork would fit in.

Pay close attention to the "Editor's Remarks" section of the market listings. Here you will find special advice from the editors of that publication for submitting material. If your work does not meet their requirements, look for a market that does. Inappropriate submissions are not only frustrating and time-consuming for the editor, they are a waste of time and postage for you.

5. Understand that artwork and written work must each be good on their own before either will be accepted.

What this means is that terrific pictures or photos will rarely convince an editor to accept a poorly written article, story, or poem. That holds true the other way around, too. If either your artwork or writing is of poor quality, it's generally better to submit just the one you are better at. If an editor is interested, he will make arrangements for suitable illustrations or photographs on his own. Or if you enjoy illustrating, he might send you someone else's story to illustrate.

There are exceptions. However, this normally only happens when one of the elements is just a little weaker in quality than the other, in which case the stronger element might be good enough to persuade the editor to accept both. When in doubt, refer to number one above: *send only your very best.*

6. If you are interested in illustrating someone else's story, photocopy some examples (three or four is enough) of your *best* work and submit them with a cover letter indicating your desire to be considered for future assignments.

There are three things to keep in mind when selecting examples of your work to send. One; choose a medium that is acceptable to the market. For instance, if they expect line drawings, send them examples of a line drawing you have done. Two; if you can and like to draw various things such as people and animals, include examples that show that you can do both. If you prefer to draw only animals, then only send examples of animals. If you like to draw both real and imaginary animals, then send a sample of each. Three; choose examples that represent your ability to *interpret* a story, poem, or article. One way to do this is by selecting a piece previously published in that market and create one or more illustrations that show how you might have handled the same assignment. Another way is to include a manuscript that you have written, along with several illustrations that relate to it. (Note: Be tactful in your letter. Do not say that you can draw better than someone that they have already published. Just say, "Enclosed are some examples of my work, based on the story, 'Ghosts and Goblins' that appeared in your March 1988 issue.")

In addition, before submitting examples and offering to illustrate for a market, decide if you will have the time to follow through with an assignment if you get one. Plus, be honest with yourself. Can you create a drawing from an idea in your mind, or have all your drawings been copies of other artists' work? Editors want and, for legal purposes, *need* original artwork. It's just as wrong to plagiarize a piece of artwork as it is to plagiarize someone else's written manuscript.

7. Don't create artwork or shoot pictures just in the hopes of getting something published or accepted for display.

As professional artist Kevin Berlin puts it, "Be true to yourself." This applies even when you hope to illustrate someone else's stories. The examples you select or create to send in with your request to be an illustrator should reflect your style, talents, and creativity. Do not create just what you *think* an editor or art director wants, but what is important to you.

8. Be sure to send a self-addressed envelope with enough postage attached so that an editor can return your work to you if it is not accepted. This is known as a SASE — self-addressed, stamped envelope.

Unlike manuscripts, some editors will also use your SASE to return your original artwork once it has appeared in print, or after the showing. Most of the listings in this *Guide* say whether or not to include a SASE. Also check for that information on the tip sheets. When a market says that submissions are not returned, you do not need to include a SASE.

Entering Contests

When entering an art or a photography contest, be sure to follow all the stated rules *exactly*. If a contest says you may submit only one piece of work in each category, do not send them two for each category. They may both be disqualified. And you'll lose any money you may have sent for an entry fee without any possibility of winning.

Pay attention to any special rules and restrictions regarding who may enter and with what type of work. For instance, many juried art contests sponsored by local, regional, and national art councils or organizations limit participation to just women, artists over eighteen, minority groups, artists from a certain state, etc. Your entry will be ignored if you attempt to submit something inappropriately.

Most contests have a coordinator who opens and reviews entries to see that all the rules have been followed and that each entry contains all of the proper identification, forms, and fees. Only those entries that have followed all the rules will be sent on to the judge or judges.

Don't be a loser before you get started.

Entering contests can be an exciting and rewarding experience. To boost your chances of winning, follow the advice and suggestions below.

1. Send for a complete list of the contest rules, regulations, and eligibility requirements.

Unfortunately, space does not allow for all the rules for every contest to be listed in this book. It is best to send a self-addressed stamped envelope (SASE) to receive the rules.

2. Follow all the rules exactly.

This includes how your work should be presented, such as whether it needs to be framed or matted. Note also whether you are to send original artwork or slides *of* your artwork. For photography, note the proper format, such as color or black and white, plus the size. On all entries pay attention to where you are supposed to put your name, address, etc., as well as the acceptable mailing format such as flat, rolled in a mailing tube, or boxed, and whether you are to include a written description of your piece, which includes the medium you chose to work in, or for photographs, the film speed and camera settings you used.

If the rules do not give specific guidelines for this information, follow the standard formats provided in this book for submitting material to an editor.

3. Don't forget to include any entry fees or required forms.

Some contests for young people request that a parent, guardian, or teacher include a *signed* statement verifying that the entry has been created entirely by the young person himself. Sometimes, you will need to sign a similar statement yourself. Be sure to include these if they are required.

4. Take care to send only finished artwork.

For lined drawings that may mean taking the time to erase (using a gum eraser) any pencil sketch lines that still show. When using chalk, charcoal, and some other mediums, you may want to seal the picture with a special fixative.

View your artwork objectively. Does it represent the best you can do? Is it truly "finished" or could it use a bit more shading; a little more, or even a little less, detail? Check the source and direction of light your artwork suggests and make sure that highlights and shadows fall realistically.

5. Don't limit yourself to contests designed just for young people.

Many talented artists and photographers have placed or won in contests open to adults. However, understand that you have the best chance of winning in contests or categories open to young people only.

6. If your entry is a combination of written text and artwork or photographs, try reviewing winning entries from previous years.

This is particularly useful where written text, such as a story book, is concerned. Yet, don't let this stop you from entering something truly different or unique. Remember, judges often change from year to year. And just because someone hasn't tried or won with a unique entry, doesn't mean yours won't. For example, in 1989, Amity Gaige entered a collection of poems, prose, and photographs in Landmark Editions *Written & Illustrated by . . . Awards Contest* instead of the traditional story and illustrations. She won first place in her age category.

7. Don't be discouraged if you don't win.

Most contests award prizes for only first, second, and third place. Some also name a number of honorable mention winners. A judge, like you, has his personal likes and dislikes. Out of the many entries, a judge must choose only a few, and sometimes just one. What he selects as best is partly determined by what he personally likes best. Another judge, or editor, may like your work better.

A Word About Rejection

It takes more to become a published young artist than enthusiasm and talent. Whether you are just an artist or also like to write, you must be aware of the many opportunities open to you. There may even be times when you want to share your work with the public because you believe in the high quality it represents. In that case you'll want to consider *suggesting* opportunities in areas where there have never been opportunities before. Talk to librarians, store managers, or even bank executives in your neighborhood to see if they'd be willing to give you space to display your work. Participate in local art fairs. Discuss possible opportunities at neighborhood galleries.

Look for opportunities to share your work in conjunction with other activities, especially those sponsored by schools, churches, and community groups.

When dealing with editors, remember that acceptance or rejection is sometimes determined by factors other than whether the person to whom you submitted material actually *likes* your work or not. Many of the same considerations that affect whether manuscripts are accepted apply to art and photographs, too. These include: the time needed by a publication to print an issue; the space available for illustrations and photos; how much material is submitted; the number of pieces that have already been accepted for publication; and the personal preferences of the editors, staff, and judges. Something that affects art and photographers much more than writing is the total cost and time involved to reproduce work in publishable form. Printing pictures and photographs in full-color is very expensive, and if four-color separation techniques are used, it is also very time-consuming. However, as more of the actual processes involved become computerized, some of the cost and time are being reduced.

Rejection is never a fun experience. But it does help to put it in perspective. The editor, art director, or judge has not rejected you personally (though it may feel like it for awhile!). He has simply picked someone else's work that better suited his needs at that moment — much like you might consider one poster over another of equal price and quality.

You may be lucky to have your work accepted or awarded a prize with your first attempt. Then again, you may need to submit work, sometimes even the *same* work, many times before, finally, something you have created is accepted. Never be discouraged. With practice your work will get better and better, and so will your chances of having it shared with the public.

Be careful not to set the wrong goals for yourself. An artist whose only goal is to have his work published, win a prize, or be displayed in a gallery, will likely experience many more disappointments than will an artist or photographer who hopes to be successful one day but whose motivation and goal, in the meantime, is to become a better artist or photographer.

Take the time now to turn to the special chapter called "Young Artists in Print." There you will find profiles of eight young artists, ranging in age from nine to eighteen, who have already had material published. There is also a profile of a "former" young artist who at twenty-five has begun to establish a career as a professional artist. Listen carefully to what they have to say. Their experiences may help you.

The "Editors Are Real People Too" chapter will introduce you to eight editors and contest sponsors and will give you a behind-the-scenes look into what they look for in the material they select. A teacher who has worked with his students as they produce documentary films is also profiled. His viewpoints are valid because for many young people, in many ways, a teacher or parent *is* the first editor that a young person works with. The helpful advice and suggestions from all of the adults profiled can be useful when submitting your work to other markets and contests as well.

I'd like to hear about you and your experiences as a young artist or photographer. Perhaps I'll include a profile of you in the next edition of Market *Guide for Young Artists and Photographers. Send your letters, questions, and comments to me at 2151 Hale Road, Sandusky, Michigan 48471.*

CHAPTER TWO
Young Artists and Photographers in Print

Ashley Callen_____

Ashley Callen, nine years old, lives in Alpharetta, Georgia with her mother, father, and two sisters, Courtney and Melanie, seven and eight. One of her drawings was published in Youth View, *a special monthly newspaper aimed at families. It is circulated primarily in Georgia.*

I have always liked to draw, especially when I look at a pot of flowers or a painting on the wall. I like to copy it. My favorite drawing book used to be the one where you make different animals by putting shapes together like circles, triangles, cylinders. They turn out to be pretty real-looking and cute. I love to copy people in cartoon-like characters and then write a funny saying underneath it. It makes people laugh.

When I was in the first grade, I won second place in a project where I painted ducks in a pond on poster paper. That was really special because it took a long time.

I love arts and crafts — origami, making hairbows, finger painting, finger puppets, painted t-shirts, and earrings. Last week I made fifteen hairbows for my sister Courtney's birthday party favors. Last summer my friend Lauren and I sold some things in our neighborhood. I'll probably always want to do something with arts and crafts as a hobby.

*Kathryn Jessica Hull*___

Kathryn Jessica Hull, eleven, lives in Savannah, Georgia, with her mother and dad, and Sammie, her Labrador Retriever. Ever since she was very young, she has loved to read and paint, so it's not surprising that beautifully illustrated books draw her like a strong magnet. Her art teacher at Savannah Country Day School has encouraged her to take risks and to do her best, which has deepened her love of art. However, overall, Kathryn is just a typical girl who loves to read, to swim, to sing and play piano, to ride her bike, and to spend time with her friends.

I have always loved art, from my finger painting days until today with the abstract painting I'm working on. I think I'll always love it.

Art is lots of fun because you know no boundaries with it. You can use it any way you like to express your feelings or ideas. For one year I went to a water color art class directed by Sharon Saseen. She paints and has illustrated one book for children. We painted several scenes in Savannah and then went to Tybee Island to paint beach scenes. After we painted, we went for a swim. It was really neat to be able to look around at the beach, and have all of the subjects you could use right there.

In my spare time I like to use art for everyday things. For example, when a birthday or special occasion comes up, I create original cards with interesting designs made of construction paper, sequins, glitter, and whatever else I have available. I also love to decorate t-shirts with fabric paints for myself or to give as gifts.

Maybe most enjoyable for me, though, is just painting when I have the urge or the time. I like watercolor and tempera paints equally because they produce different effects. Usually, I have a place or object in view so I can paint a natural scene or a still life. But sometimes I just try new techniques for the fun of it, like sprinkling salt on watercolor pictures and seeing how it changes the color and the outlines of things.

My art teacher at school is Sharon Renfrow. She is an extremely talented artist and does a great job teaching. One day Ms. Renfrow came into the art room with a new project. She explained that what we were going to do was make an abstract painting. She would hold up five pictures of people and animals; then we would draw each in semi-blind contour. (That is when you look at something and draw it without picking your pencil up off the paper but looking at your drawing only occasionally.) She said we needed to draw the lines fairly far apart and have some of them go off the page so we wouldn't have one big glob in the center of the paper.

After we finished our drawings, we were to choose a color scheme to paint our drawing in. I chose an analogous color scheme, four colors right next to each other on the color wheel. So I drew up the pencil sketch and got to work. It took me lots longer to do mine than the other kids. I was using a very small brush to paint carefully in small spaces — I guess I'm a perfectionist. I finally had to put it aside so I could start the next project.

A few weeks later, Ms. Renfrow asked me to finish my painting. I thought it was so I could be graded, so I finished it. When I was done, I was proud of myself. It had taken a long time, but I had enjoyed it. Ms. Renfrow took my painting and turned it in to *Spring Tides*, a literary magazine with writing and art by children from all over the East Coast. It was published! Then Ms. Renfrow told me what she had done. I was surprised and pleased. Later Mrs. Smith, my language arts teachers, told me she had been contacted by a company that wanted to publish a book about young illustrators. It made me proud that someone else would want to recognize my work.

Although in the future I'd like to be a veterinarian, a pediatrician, or a surgeon, art will always be a hobby and personal pleasure. Perhaps if I'm good enough, it will even be a source of income. I have some advice for other artists: Sometimes you try and you don't make it; sometimes you do. But when you don't make it, don't give up!

*Emily Davidson*_____

In addition to drawing for her own pleasure and entering art contests, eleven-year-old Emily Davidson of Billings, Montana, also likes to design greeting cards. Extra cards are duplicated inexpensively at a local print shop. Sometimes her older sister Lauren helps color in the covers of the cards or writes something inside. A few years ago, the family used one of Emily's cards as their official Christmas card, which was sent to family and friends back in Michigan.

Moving to Montana has inspired Emily's art and writing. Though Webster's New World Dictionary *lists the spelling of the cone-shaped animal skin hut commonly used by the Plains Indians as tepee, Emily has chosen to use the local Native American Indian spelling of tipi in her essay.*

I have always been interested in art because my parents were also interested and they always had the supplies and encouraged me to draw. I like to observe nature and later sketch it. Being outside inspires me to draw because some things are just so beautiful I don't want to forget them, so I draw them.

When I was two years old my mom would come home from art class and start to draw for hours. I would draw for hours right along with her.

Ever since I've been living in Montana, I have been getting more and more inspired to draw because there are beautiful mountains, colorful sunsets, and prairies. We've done many things in Montana, like going to a paleontology camp, hiking in the mountains, and camping. Last summer I slept in a tipi at Crow Fair, which is one of the largest gatherings of Native Americans in the United States.

Some day I hope to be a professional artist. I especially like to draw rabbits.

*Marisa Fiordalisi*_____

One of the things that makes twelve-year-old Marisa Fiordalisi of East Norwich, New York, so successful is that she is always creating new work. Plus, she is lucky to have a teacher and a parent who not only encourage her, but help her find new markets and contests, and send things in. But even with double the help and encouragement, Marisa wouldn't be successful at all if she didn't practice her art and writing — trying new ideas, and having the confidence to re-submit work that has been rejected elsewhere.

Not all of Marisa's experiences have been wonderful. But she hasn't let the disappointments get her down, or stop her from trying again.

I have loved to draw ever since I was five years old and began sketching fashions in second grade. By fourth grade I had started creating my own, original cartoon characters and was accepted into our school's G.I.F.T.E.D. program, which is taught by Mr. Richard Siegelman.

During the past two years, Mr. Siegelman has helped me enter many contests, which not only gave me a chance to use my artistic talents, but helped me develop my writing skills as well. In fact, it was Mr. Siegelman who felt that my writing was as good, if not better, than my artwork, and he has sent many of my poems and stories to various publications.

Encouraged by my many successes in the G.I.F.T.E.D. program, and because of the tremendous amount of support and interest I got from Mr. Siegelman and my mother, my dream is to combine my love of art and writing and become a cartoonist, or a writer and illustrator of children's books when I grow up. My cartoon characters include Ellen Maloney, Pedro and Margarita, the Fuzzies, the Short People, the Happy Holiday Characters, and many others. I think that drawing and writing are wonderful because I get to express my thoughts and feelings in a way that is special, unique, and, hopefully, appealing to other people.

In the Fall of 1988, I entered a Mother's Day Card Contest sponsored by Kentucky Fried Chicken and *Good Housekeeping* magazine. The grand prize winner receives a monetary award in addition to having his or her card printed and sold. I was notified in January that I was a finalist, and by March I had become the New York State winner. Although I was not published, I did receive a home computer and was invited to the awards ceremony held at the Empire State Building in May, where I met actress Markie Post and some of the other contest winners. It was still quite an accomplishment since this contest draws over 600,000 entries and 40,000 of them were from New York State.

In 1988, I also became one of six students to serve on the Student Advisory Board of Gifted Children *Monthly* for one year. We were introduced in the March issue and my picture, along with an excerpt from my essay about my interest in cartooning was printed in the *Spinoff* section. My circus characters were printed in the June issue to announce a contest that invited kids to invent the "Spin-Off Gang." My idea for children to create their own cartoon characters became a regular department. For fun I decided to do caricatures of all the student advisors. These were printed the following December when it came time to pick six new students for the job.

"Pumpkin and the Gang Go On Vacation" was my very first story. It was about my first cartoon characters, the Fuzzies. It was entered in the Young Writers' Foundation contest, and although it was not among the work published in their 1988 *Rainbow Collection*, it was one of 500 finalists out of over 10,000 entries. I was very happy at the thought that somebody actually like my characters.

Some of my other work has been published in *Children's Album, Knowledge Master Open Newspaper, Undersea Journal, Creative Kids* magazine, and *The McGuffey Writer*, as well as other places.

My mother's boss (she works at a pharmacy) was so impressed by my accomplishments that he asked me to do a cartoon ad for him to launch the Christmas season. I drew Santa shopping at the drugstore. It was printed in the Sunday edition of *Newsday*, Long Island's major newspaper. That project was not only fun, but it was also quite an honor and my first "paying" job.

In one of the most enjoyable contests I ever entered I had to create an original calendar. My calendar was complete with a cover, plus a picture and poem for each of the twelve months. Both Mr. Siegelman and I thought it was among my best work and we were both very disappointed when it didn't win. Later, *Reflections* printed nine of the poems and pictures along with a story about me.

"Ellen and the Magic Wand," a story about my favorite character Ellen Maloney, did not win Raintree's "Publish a Book" contest either. However, a slightly longer version did win first place in a contest sponsored by the National Story League. It felt wonderful to see it in *Story Art*, their magazine for storytellers.

Ellen is my favorite character for several reasons, but mainly because I feel that many young children can relate to this seven year old and her "Five BIG Problems." Winning this contest made me so happy because I had used my Ellen character in so many contests, yet she was never a "winner" until then. It made me glad that somebody finally liked her, especially since I have so many big dreams for Ellen.

I continue to enter many contests and submit both my writing and art to various markets. Many of these places have *thousands* of entries submitted. Although I try to remain hopeful, I realize how difficult it is to win sometimes.

Win or lose, published or unpublished, I will always love to draw and write. I like creating my own characters and writing stories about them for my own enjoyment. I like writing poetry just for fun. I feel that I have been very lucky to have accomplished so much at such an early age. I am always surprised and pleased when people like my work, yet sometimes I feel that some of my best work goes unnoticed. I have come to understand that the same work can be accepted or rejected, loved or hated, depending upon an editor's needs or interests. Mr. Siegelman has taught me that even when I lose, it's not because my work isn't good, but because someone else's might be better or more suitable for a particular publication.

I plan to continue working hard to develop my talents so that I can become a successful writer and artist someday. I realize that the competition is stiff, but I am definitely not afraid to try.

Elizabeth Haidle_____

Paul Haidle_____

Paul, thirteen, and Elizabeth, fifteen, are just two of three very talented siblings from the Portland, Oregon area. Seventeen-year-old Jonathan, now a student at Portland Community College, won a second place award in the 1987 MADD *magazine poster contest. However, Jonathan's true love is music, while Paul and Elizabeth prefer art.*

In addition to illustrating a cover for the 1990 Winter issue of Shoe Tree, *Paul has also provided five illustrations of apes and men for a story* Shoe Tree *published about a shipwreck. In 1989, he won second place for his age group in the Landmark Editions "Written & Illustrated By ... Awards Contest."*

"Paul loves animals," says Shoe Tree *editor Sheila Cowing. "What drew me to his work originally was a raccoon he drew when he was nine. But he is very versatile."*

Elizabeth placed first in her category in the same "Written & Illustrated By ..." contest. Unlike Paul's realistic animal drawings, her story and art featured a fictional character named Elmer, "the grumpiest Elfkin in the woods."

In the following separate essays, you'll get a glimpse of the joint encouragement these siblings received. However, also note how Paul and Elizabeth infuse their own personalities and interests into their individual art. And note the different advice each decided was most important to share.

Paul Haidle

Art has always existed in our family here in Portland. There was never an excuse not to draw; pens, paper, markers, and just about everything you could think of were put in my hand ever since I can remember. My parents had boxes of markers, countless sheets of paper, and lots of paper and places to scribble in and on, including the bathroom wall. I can remember in kindergarten (my parents kept me home) making pictures ranging from our backyard flowers to the typical boy's war scenes. My parents thought all my art work was great! They gave me lots of encouragement. (Plus storage room for saving my works of art!)

The most important thing that kept me in art were those small, local, coloring contests in kids' magazines or at grocery stores. My mother, who stayed at home with us, would always bring contests home for us to color. Usually leaving them to the final deadline, I would quickly draw in last minute details and hand it to my mom, who would rush them to the grocery store. The prizes I won weren't too big, but they soon built up to quite a bit.

As I got older I began entering national contests. The ones in Young American newspapers were my favorite. Instead of just coloring in some outlined drawing a store manager tried to do, I now could draw my own ideas. My creativity grew with every contest. Even the contests I lost didn't stop me (often I wouldn't even remember that I had entered them). I also learned that it's sometimes not how good you can draw, but *HOW* you draw it. That's what creativity is. That's why I suggest that kids get their parents to help them find a couple of contests for them to enter. It doesn't matter if you don't win; your creativity, and drawing ability, will grow anyway. But be sure to make a photocopy of your work, so you can keep examples of the things you've done.

The next step in my life involved getting my works published. I especially enjoyed doing sketches of animals I found in *National Geographic* magazines. So I sent one of my sketches of a raccoon in a tree to a contest for students in Oregon and it was published in *Treasures 2*. It was also published in *Shoe Tree* magazine. *Shoe Tree* also accepted a watercolor scene I did for one of its covers and I also did an illustration for another student-author's story.

At first it didn't seem very exciting to have my drawings published, but when I thought about all the people who would be looking at my drawings, I mused that I actually might become "famous" (in a school or two). I soon realized getting something published is one of the best rewards you can receive. I encourage everyone to enter one of your pictures, sketches, or writings to a contest where you can have a chance to get it published. Not only will you have an everlasting copy of your work, but you can get as many [copies] as you want.

The most difficult and challenging project I've done was to write and illustrate my own book, which I entered in Landmark Edition's "*1989 National Written & Illustrated By ... Contest.*" My book was about three animals — a beaver, a skunk, and a turtle — who help each other survive a challenging journey down the river. I won a second place scholarship award of $2,000. Now I enjoy making author/illustrator visits to grade schools in Oregon and encouraging students in their creativity, and giving them suggestions on how to get their work published.

I sometimes talk to parents, too, and encourage them to take a little time and find something for their child to enter. Encourage them, and let them know how proud you are of them to start and finish something so wonderful. Who knows? It might keep them out of trouble, or at least away from the TV for a while.

Elizabeth Haidle

Ever since I can remember, I have been drawing. My parents kept all my old artwork, from sketchbook pages filled with comical scribbles and childish attempts at watercolor, to sloppy sculptures.

My parents always encouraged me to try new things, like Craypas™ and baking clay, or poetry and illustrated short stories. All three of us kids had journals that we would write and draw in when we went on vacations or adventures. Our parents helped us jot down things we'd want to remember and then we would draw pictures of what we did. Sometimes on evenings, we would make up songs or stories while our parents wrote them down for us. The most fun part for me was illustrating them, of course.

Then, in grade school, I had some wonderful teachers who encouraged doing creative extra-credit assignments. In the fourth and fifth grades, my best friend and I worked on a variety of projects, such as making research collages with magazine pictures and writing about them, or constructing picture books about wild forest animals, or even writing funny plays about a snobby fat lady and her clumsy maid, which we put on for the class.

And ever since kindergarten, I've won lots of coloring and drawing contests that my parents searched out and encouraged me to enter. I look back in appreciation at those grocery stores and our local library, which provided opportunities for kids to express themselves creatively through art work. One contest that stands out in my mind was in third grade. Our local newspaper encouraged kids to "Design Your Own Christmas Card." I won first prize and got my picture in the paper, plus a cash award.

One important impression happened at the age of five when I saw Steven Kellogg in action. He illustrated one of his stories as he told it and I was fascinated watching him fill up pages of paper with line drawing. But fifth grade was when I first made up my elf characters that later would become a published book of my own. I still remember lying on the floor drawing a king and queen elf with a baby princess. I drew city and country elves and decided to make their homes in mushrooms and give them snails for pets.

In sixth grade, I felt I wasn't being challenged enough in school, so I home-schooled the last quarter or so. My mom suggested that I work on some sort of project to show my teachers in case they wondered if I was actually doing anything at home. So I decided to write and illustrate my own book about the elf characters that I had made up. I spent hours looking at books on mushrooms, forests, snails, and insects as I made up an Elfkin world.

Though my parents thought it was good enough to be published, I never thought it would be possible until I was all grown up at the age of twenty or thirty. Sure, authors who came to our school told us that we could start writing and publishing now, but they didn't get anything printed until they were adults. So I kept my book around and occasionally thought about redoing it in the future until one day, in the eighth grade, my mom found an article in the newspaper telling about a girl who had entered a contest that published your book if you won.

The 1988 contest deadline was only a month away, so I quickly launched into rewriting and illustrating, working busily after school until the last hour of the deadline. I didn't know what to expect. I heard there were thousands of entries, so I figured I didn't stand much of a chance. But I thought I could just take it around and try other publishers if I didn't win. So I was very surprised to find out in September that I had won!

Lately, I've been visiting grade schools and talking about how I got work published and how they can write their own original story and illustrate it, too. I describe the writing process to them after a brief slide show, and at the end I show them how to "brain-storm" and illustrate their own creative characters. The kids love to watch me draw and they all get excited about illustrating too. Even though it's been tough missing several days of school a semester and making up all the work, it's worth the experience because the kids get so inspired when they see others their own age who are successful at doing something that they themselves could do just as well.

Now, this past semester of my sophomore year in high school, I'm involved in an independent study program where you can work on an approved project and receive credit for it. I chose to write and illustrate another book. The most fun kind of book to do, I decided, would be an alphabet book. So I've been re-working and re-drawing animal characters such as Swanky, Suave Swans, Burping Baboons, Hyper Hens, Time-worn Tortoises, and Delicate, Dreamily-dressed Does.

I've also grown artistically this year. I have found that if I expand into other areas of art that I haven't tried before, and I practice them, that I can become good at them. Usually people just stick to one thing and say they are only good at one specialty, like drawing horses. They never try drawing people or sculpting things because they don't like the feeling of failure. But if you persevere and try hard enough, it'll pay off. You will get that wonderful feeling of artistic creativity, experienced in a harder, more difficult area for you.

*Janelle Colby*_____

Though Janelle Colby, eighteen, of Sandusky, Michigan, has always been a very active artist, she isn't motivated very often to pursue market or contest opportunities. However, she did enter a special poster contest during her last year in high school. Sponsored by the county intermediate school district, the theme was "The Year 2000 — Attack and Beyond." Janelle's dramatic drawing of Earth being literally torn apart by neglectful Man won first place in the high school category.

While she intends to pursue art, it will most likely be only as a hobby, one that not only gives her immense satisfaction but helps to relieve stress.

As far back as I can remember, I have loved to draw. My mother always kept me well supplied with a wide variety of art materials. Since my brothers were half-grown when I came along, and since I lived far out in the country, I primarily had to provide my own entertainment.

For me, art always took precedence over other childhood activities. Consequently, I got many hours of practice gleefully experimenting at my table, which was always heaped high with paper, crayons, markers, pencils, paints, charcoals, and works in various stages of development.

I had no formal art training until my high school years. In our rural area there were simply no opportunities in or out of school for art instruction, so I worked on my own with my only feedback being my family's praise. Mrs. Lynn Jacobs, my high school art teacher for four years, has been my mentor, technical advisor, and morale booster. She made art class so much fun with her sunny attitude, positive comments, and enthusiasm. I discovered that art class was a great stress reliever in an otherwise stringent academic schedule. I looked forward to it every day.

Art makes me feel good. Maybe that's because I've been successful and have gotten a lot of positive strokes for what I've done. My mother, an elementary school teacher, often had me draw things for her bulletin boards at school, and in some ways I became "Artist in Residence" at my high school — making posters for the National Honor Society, the Red Cross bloodmobile, the cheerleaders, and other groups and programs. My mother has framed and hung an oil, a pen and ink, and a charcoal of mine — her favorite pieces — in our home.

Because I always thought of art as a hobby, I really never considered doing anything competitive with it until my senior year. Even then I was concerned that the stress of competition would take the fun out of what I've always loved. I was encouraged by my art teacher and my family to enter a county-wide poster competition sponsored by our intermediate school district. I guess this competition came at just the right time, since I was feeling particularly confident following the awarding of a $1500 art scholarship given to me by the college I will attend in the fall.

The theme of this year's "First Impressions" competition was "The Year 2000, Attack And Beyond." When I first considered the theme absolutely nothing came to mind. So I let it go. Actually, I think I gave up on entering altogether since I had no idea where to go with it. But every once in a while, I'd find myself thinking about it again, and surprisingly, something began taking form in my mind. I messed around with some sketches. Then one unusually quiet weekend, I went to work.

I had decided to depict the earth being literally torn apart by mankind's neglect and abuse. I chose pen and ink as my medium with some sponge work in the background. For something like this, black and white is so much more dramatic than color. I worked intensely most of Saturday, put on the finishing touches on Sunday, entered it on Monday, and then forgot it in the excitement of senior activities.

I was happy that I won the "First Impressions" competition even though the reward was mainly honorary. (The winners were given medals.) However, I had fun doing the poster. It was a challenge.

Beginning a new art project is for me very exciting. Whether I'm working from a photograph or three-dimensional models, I immediately begin to speculate on how I'm going to interpret the various details. I can actually feel myself doing this. I maintain intense concentration while working, probably because the work itself is highly motivating. If I get stuck while working on a project or don't know how to begin a piece, I quit working on it for a day or two. Inevitably this fallow period is followed by a new spurt of creativity and solutions suddenly present themselves to me. I never give up on a project, always finishing it even if I'm not always satisfied with the results.

Although I'm not going to pursue art as a career, I know it will always be a part of my life. I love art and so will always find someway to express myself creatively.

*Amity Gaige*_____

Amity Gaige, seventeen and of Reading, Pennsylvania, won first place in the 1989 National Written & Illustrated By ... Awards Contest *for the fourteen to nineteen age category. She was sixteen at the time. Her entry,* We Are A Thunderstorm, *is a collection of her poems dramatically illustrated with photographs she took herself.*

More than forty of Amity's poems, short stories, essays, plays, and photographs have appeared in Shoe Tree, Merlyn's Pen, Cricket Magazine, *and other publications. Her work has also won many national first place awards including the* Cricket Magazine *Poetry Contest (1983, 1986, 1988); the National Association for Young Writers Poetry Contest in 1987; The 1988 NAYW Short Story Contest; and the 1990 Scholastic Short Story Competition. In 1986, Amity was selected Scholar of the Week in Humanities at the Johns Hopkins University Center for the Advancement of Academically Talented Youth. She was also awarded a full scholarship in creative writing from the Pennsylvania Governor's School for Arts, held the summer of 1990 at Mercyhurst College, in Erie, Pennsylvania. She enjoys ballet and jazz dancing, and is active in many school organizations.*

One of the ingredients fueling Amity's success (besides a lot of hard work) is her willingness to take chances, like illustrating her book with photographs when everyone else she knew drew pictures. She also speaks out on issues others shy away from. "I try to be politically aware and active," she says in We Are A Thunderstorm, *"and I have marched for women's rights and civil rights in Washington, DC. I believe it is our responsibility to leave the world a little better than we found it. I hope my writing helps to open eyes and open minds."*

While illustrating my book of poetry, *We Are A Thunderstorm,* with photography, I ran into a funny misconception. Some other young authors, who were illustrating books through the same publisher, complained that "the girl who is taking pictures has it easy." They thought that their drawings and paintings were incomparably harder to do, and that all I had to do was push a button!

While anyone can take a photograph, not everyone can take a

good photograph. The fact is, a good photograph is a happy collision of many, many things.

Let me cite an example. I wrote a poem called "Hanging On" for which I needed a picture of a little southern farm boy hanging onto his father's pants leg at the sight of a tornado. I know no little southern farm boys, nor did Pennsylvania in the dead of winter look like the South. Yet after lots of phone calls, I found a family who could help me. It took a half hour to get to their farm, and all the while I was hoping the sun would stay out and wondering whether or not I should use my tripod. When I got there, I had to establish a relationship with the subjects. I needed my little farm boy to feel comfortable in front of my camera. This was complicated by the fact that he had to wear just a thin shirt in the freezing weather in order to look "southern." I needed to decide how I wanted him to sit, what expression I wanted on his face, which backdrop looked best. And in the middle of all that, my camera popped open by accident and half a roll of film was exposed.

Geez.

But what I got were a few good photographs, and I was proud of them. Good photography, not just any regular "push of a button," is an illusive and beautiful art form. It is life in its realest state. Though a photographer struggles against many odds, when he or she captures a "good photo" it is magical.

I don't really blame those other artists for their misconception about photography. Not until I myself experimented with it did I gain the immense appreciation I hold for it now. When I go into museums now, I am just as awed by the great photographic works as I am by the Monets and Picassos. Paintings are magical and creative, but the intrinsic beauty of the world is best seen in a "good" photo. Try it yourself. I think you'll see what I mean.

Kevin Berlin_____

*In the winter of 1983, Kevin Berlin, of Poto-
mac, Maryland, then a junior in high school,
was selected as one of the nation's seven top
visual artists in the "ARTS Recognition and
Talent Search." Though he had won awards
for his art before, this competition marked an
important turning point in his perception of himself as an artist. Art became
more than a passionate hobby; it became a career to pursue.*

*Now twenty-five, Kevin considers himself a full-time artist, surviving
primarily by income and grants related to his work, though he is quick to
point out that his parents have been very supportive – including financially
– when things get tight. His story and advice to young artists is included
here as both incentive and proof that serious young artists can and do grow
up to be professional artists. His sister Danielle, twenty-two, and brother
Noah, just sixteen, are also successful artists. While Kevin says the theme of
his work is America, Danielle prefers romanticism with Italian overtones,
and Noah, who studies Japanese art, has his own business. A third sibling,
Justin, twenty-six, is studying filmmaking.*

*Kevin credits part of his success to his versatility as an artist. He works
in a variety of mediums including painting, sculpture, drawing, and wood
cutouts. "Something artists often forget is that they must promote their
work," says Kevin. "It's the only way you're going to be successful." He adds
that if you present yourself as a legitimate artist, you'll be perceived as one.*

One of my earliest memories is decorating my own "turtle" cake on
my fifth birthday. I spent hours copying pictures from encyclope-
dias and adding illustrations to my school projects. My teachers
gave me lots of compliments on my work and by fifth grade my
mom signed me up to take art lessons outside of school.

In second grade I won a prize at an art contest sponsored by a
local bank; a check for one dollar. Soon I won some national
poster contests like Baskin-Robbins "Ice Cream is a Birthday Fantasy" contest, and Scotts Lawn and Garden's "Draw a Super Vegetable Contest." My prizes included thirty-one free ice cream cones
and a twenty-five dollar savings bond. It never occurred to me that I

might have some special talent. I was just lucky and also I worked very hard on my entries.

At the end of elementary school I began to notice for the first time that my classmates considered me a "good artist." One day, while I was copying the Mona Lisa in my junior high art class, my teacher Mr. Shampain came up to me. He watched for a while, shook his head several times and said with a wide grin, "Kevin, my boy, you should have taken music." Kidding aside, I knew Mr. Shampain secretly liked my work because he began displaying it in a glass case in the hallway outside the art room.

In junior high I also began my own comic strip, "Bonad the Philosopher." It was about a peculiar traveling man who was always trying to get himself out of trouble by quoting the great philosophers. The strip's success led me to become graphics editor of *The Panthers Print,* our school newspaper. So I found myself entrusted with power and authority. I loved giving out assignments to my staff, and drawing editorial cartoons (my favorite showed a student collapsing after eating the cafeteria food). Eventually, I did the yearbook cover my senior year and made posters for my friends who were running for student government offices. Outside of school I started taking college classes at The Corcoran School of Art in nearby Washington, DC. At fifteen, I found myself in a class filled with grown-ups drawing from a nude model. My new heroes were Michelangelo and Rembrandt.

In high school I really began to take advantage of my abilities. I was blessed with a brilliant art teacher who helped me to challenge my strengths and focus on my weaknesses. Rather than teach me how to work in someone else's style, he taught me how to discover my own. My ability to express myself through drawings and paintings improved dramatically. I became Graphics Editor of our award-winning high school newspaper, *The Black and White,* and also began to pounce on every artwork opportunity that came by. I made illustrations and covers for my academic teachers, school organizations, the student government, the P.T.A., the yearbook, and even the school telephone directory. In addition, I entered every art contest under the sun and won prizes in such things as a "gold key" at the "Scholastic Art Awards" and "best double-page layout" at the Temple University Press Tournament.

Even up until this time I didn't consider my abilities of any special significance. I just always did what I loved doing — making things and sharing them with other people. In terms of my future I merely assumed I would become a doctor or a lawyer or something because that's what you're supposed to do. I never thought I could spend my life doing something that I really enjoyed doing.

A dramatic turning point came in my life when I was flown down to Florida as a finalist for the "National ARTS Recognition and Talent Search" sponsored by the National Foundation for Advancement in the Arts. All I had to do was send twenty slides of my work and the next thing I knew I had won $4000 in scholarship "encouragement" money and was being honored by the President on the White House lawn. I never imaged something like this could happen to me. It was then I decided to concentrate my energy on my art.

I decided if my work was ever going to say something about the world, I had better know something about the world first. After four years at Yale University, one year at the Slade School of Fine Arts in London, and travels to Africa, China, and Europe I thought I was finally ready to show my work in a local art gallery. Boy, was I in for a shock. I remember one art gallery owner who asked me if she could be honest about her opinion of my portfolio. I said, "Of course." She then proceeded to tell me that I seemed like a nice young man, but that there was basically nothing original about my work, that it did nothing for her, and that I should consider starting completely over from scratch.

This kind of response can be very upsetting. It didn't take long to learn that everyone has an opinion. Instead of quitting, I re-interpreted negative comments as a challenge to work even harder. Several months and many gallery visits later I asked a different gallery owner if she "could think of an appropriate place for me to show my work." She paused for a moment, then said, "I know where you could show your work . . . you could show it right here." I nearly bit off my lower lip. Hers was one of my favorite galleries in the whole Washington, DC area!

Berlin's Ten Rules to Live By

1. Show your work everywhere and every time you can. No opportunity is too small. Every drop helps turn the mill.

2. Keep making new work. Every day. If you're going to be an Olympic athlete, you've got to train.

3. Keep learning more. Continue to educate yourself. If you like ancient Greek art, see it in person. If there's a painter who interests you, find that painter's work in a museum, the library, and a bookstore. If you want to improve your figure drawing or learn to carve stone, sign up for a class or workshop. Actively seek the answers to your questions.

4. Keep a sketchbook or "idea" book. Carry it with you every day. You must be ready to draw or write at any moment. It is difficult to plan inspiration.

5. Be lucky. Or at least make the odds work in your favor. If you enter ten contests, you have a better chance for success than if you only enter one.

6. Treat your best work as if it belongs in a museum. Damaged work makes a weaker impression. I've seen lots of beautiful pieces that are wrinkled or torn. If you don't show respect for your work why should someone else? Invest in a portfolio case or make your own with heavy cardboard. Keep your works neat and clean.

7. Get feedback from people you respect. Sometimes you're too close to your work to make competent decisions about it. If you're not positive what to submit, or how it should be presented, get a second or even third opinion from teachers and friends who have more experience.

8. Try to understand your critics. Put yourself in their shoes. Every person has their own personal bias. By looking at their work you may find an explanation for the things they suggest. They are probably trying to help you.

9. Don't take rejection personally. Juries are not responding to you, but rather to an object, an artwork that you presented to them. Their decision is more a reflection of them and their objectives, than of you. Try again.

10. Be true to yourself. When you stop enjoying your work, you will stop working.

CHAPTER THREE
Editors are Real People, Too

Ever wonder what goes on behind the scenes of your favorite publication or contest? Would you like to know who's in charge, and what they're *really* like? Do you ever wish you could talk with someone, just the two of you alone, maybe get a few tips that would help you create winning artwork and photography? Would you like to know what criteria they use to judge what to accept or reject?

In this chapter, you'll get answers to those questions from a specially selected group of editors and contest coordinators. They'll also share additional material about their publications and contests, why and how they themselves got involved. Some will even share some embarrassing or disappointing moments from their own pasts. All this so you can get a better perspective of the opportunities within your reach as a young artist or photographer.

With each new edition of *Market Guide*, it's my pleasure to invite a different panel of editors and contest sponsors to participate. I try hard to choose people not only from a wide variety of backgrounds and markets but also several from markets and contests that seem very similar. By doing so, you'll learn to better recognize the differences as well as the similarities, because the more you understand the subtleties involved, the more successful you'll be winning an award or getting your creative work accepted by a publication.

As you read each profile keep in mind what the previous young artists had to say about *their* half of the experience. Then put two and two together and market your own winning combo. It takes two. And editors are real people, too.

William Rubel_____

Co-editor of *Stone Soup, The Magazine By Children*

William Rubel and co-founder Gerry Mandel started publishing Stone Soup *in 1973 when they were twenty-year-old students at the University of California and Santa Cruz. Over the last eighteen years, as co-editors they have read hundreds of thousands of pages of children's writing and art.*

"We love what we do," says Gerry Mandel. "It's very satisfying to be able to encourage young writers and artists by presenting the best of their work in Stone Soup."

In the following, William Rubel shares important points about submitting both artwork and writing to Stone Soup.

Gerry Mandel and I started *Stone Soup* eighteen years ago. Since then we have published over 3500 pages of writing and art by children! This is more than any other publisher in the world. Sending manuscripts to *Stone Soup* is easy. You don't have to type or copy over your writing. If you are under fourteen, just send us your work along with a self-addressed stamped envelope.

While it is easy to send us work, it isn't necessarily easy to get that work accepted. Ms. Mandel and I have very definite ideas about what our magazine should be like. *Stone Soup* is our life's work, and we only publish in it the kind of writing we like to read and the kind of art we like to look at. We also look at art, listen to music, and enjoy theater. In our own lives we look to artists — novelists, poets, critics, painters, illustrators, playwrights, musicians — to illuminate and enrich our lives. In *Stone Soup* we publish writing and art that bring something new, something fresh, something special into our lives.

The best way to get a sense of the kind of material we publish in *Stone Soup* is to read one or more issues of the magazine carefully. In fact, before sending work to any magazine, it is a good idea to read some back issues. If followed, this simple piece of advice would save many writers (and editors) a great deal of effort.

Look for *Stone Soup* in your school or public library, or write to us and order a sample copy. Read carefully. Think about what you read. Think about what you write. How is the material in *Stone Soup* similar to what you write? How is it different?

Read the poems. Observe their form. You will notice that we publish poems written in a compressively free form. You won't find any highly structured poems like haiku, cinquains, or limericks, and none of the poems rhyme. This last observation is a very important one. Approximately half of all manuscripts sent to us are poems. And of those virtually all are rhymed. In eighteen years we have only published two rhymed poems! So if you write rhymed poetry you should realize from reading *Stone Soup* that this is *not* the magazine that is likely to publish your work.

What kind of poetry do we publish? We publish poems in which the author uses a few words to express an idea, evoke a feeling, or make an observation. Poetry should be very musical. Ideally, it should use words in a fresh way. The poets published in *Stone Soup* are working towards these goals.

You will find many stories about personal experiences in *Stone Soup*. Over the years the percentage of *Stone Soup* devoted to personal experiences has significantly increased. We find that the best stories we read are written about events that mattered personally to the author. Changing schools, the death of a pet, winning a big sports event, overcoming a physical handicap, escaping from Vietnam on a boat, spending time alone in a special place — these are all examples of subjects that recur in *Stone Soup*. All of your skills at telling a story can be used when you tell your own story. The line between fact and fiction, history and the historical novel, is a wobblyline. The authors published in *Stone Soup* use their imagination plus all of their skills at plot, dialogue, and description to create interesting stories based on important moments in their own lives.

Art is a very important part of *Stone Soup*. We publish pictures in color and in black and white. Many of the stories are illustrated, and pictures and text work together to tell the story. Look at the art. What I said about poetry and writing also holds true for art. You will notice that the beautiful color pictures and the drawings are clearly inspired by careful observation of the real world. You don't find rainbows floating in the sky between two clouds. You don't find cartoon figures, smiley faces, or unicorns. You will notice, especially of the color work, that the artists use the whole page when they make their pictures. No portion of the paper is left out. Just as stories have beginnings, middles, and ends, pictures have a foreground, a middle ground, and a background. When you leave a portion of your picture blank, it is similar to leaving part of your story untold. If you like to draw and make pictures that are inspired by the wonderful things you see around you, please write to us. We are always looking for illustrators.

In conclusion, I'd like to emphasize something else that is very important for you to keep in mind. *Stone Soup* is a literary magazine. This means that, in addition to caring about what you say, we care about how you say it. As editors, the worst moments for us are when we are reading a story that meets all of our standards for subject matter and sincerity but still cannot be published because of one missing ingredient: interesting language.

Every story, poem, and book review published in *Stone Soup* is first read aloud. Only after hearing what the words sound like can we be sure we want to publish a work. What do we listen for? We listen to the music your words make. We ask ourselves, "Is the music interesting or is it getting a little boring?" We listen for the sound of an artist who is working hard to say something important as truthfully and as beautifully as possible.

David Melton_____

National Written & Illustrated by . . .
Awards Contest

David Melton is one of the most versatile and prolific people involved with writing and art today. And he is among the most enthusiastic supporters of young people and their creative efforts. His own literary work includes factual prose, analytical essays, news-reporting, magazine articles, features, short stories, poetry, and novels for both adults and children.

Mr. Melton has illustrated twelve of his own books and three by other authors. Many of his drawings and paintings have been reproduced as fine art prints, posters, puzzles, calendars, book jackets, record covers, mobiles, and note cards, and they have also been featured in national publications.

To help teachers encourage students to write and illustrate original books, he developed the highly acclaimed manual, Written and Illustrated By . . ., *which is now used in thousands of schools nationwide. He considers it his privilege to assist student winners of his contests while they put the finishing touches on their work in preparation for final production and publishing.*

I think I'm one of the luckiest persons alive because I write and illustrate books and get paid for it. But I'll tell you a secret — if I didn't get paid, I would still write and illustrate because it's so much fun to create books.

I've always loved to draw and paint. When I was in school, to my art teachers' delight and my math teachers' dismay, I drew pictures most of the time. No piece of paper was safe from my attack. My drawings filled sketch pads, notebook pages, margins of English papers, sides of spelling tests, and corners of math assignments.

I drew cartoons, portraits, caricatures of friends and enemies, and anything else that came to mind. Some drawings were serious explorations of line and color; some were hilarious; some were downright silly; and some were no more than aimless doodles that poured forth from my restless mind.

When I was a seventh grader, the editors of the school news-paper held an art contest and one of my cartoons won. It was printed in the next edition, and I became an instant school celebrity for a day. Many students stopped me in the hallway and told me how much they liked the cartoon. There were, of course, a couple of classmates who groused and said it was the worst thing they had ever seen. No matter. Through the printing of that cartoon, I had discovered a whole new world — the printed page.

I was amazed to realize that an artist can draw or paint an illustration or a cartoon, and then that piece of work can be printed hundreds, or thousands, or even millions of times, and be seen by hundreds, or thousands, or even millions of viewers. It excited me even more to consider that reproductions of an artist's work have the potential of influencing the thinking of so many people.

After I graduated from college, I worked for a number of years as a commercial artists. While I enjoyed designing and illustrating advertising brochures, I mostly wanted to illustrate books. Book designing and illustrating held a special fascination for me, and it still does. As an artist developing a book, I enjoy the opportunity to plan, mold, and create a total environment that has complete sense of beginning, middle, and end.

I am often asked what is the difference between an artist and an illustrator? The answer is simple: an artist is one who is skilled in drawing and painting, etc., and has the freedom to select his or her own subject and develop it in line, shape, and color. An illustrator is an artist, too, but his or her primary function is to represent the intent of the writer by visually interpreting the written materials. Not only do the best illustrators have the ability to remain true to an author's words — they are also adept at interjecting additional information and emphasis into a story.

The illustrator has to consider several exciting things crucial to the well-being of a book: Should he depict only what is described in the text, or should a piece of visual information be added? Which style of art best illuminates the setting and time period of the story? And how can color, line, shape, and composition emphasize the moods of the text? If the artist makes the right decisions, the illustrations won't compete with the story. Instead, they will blend with and enhance the text, never distracting the reader from the story, but encouraging that person to continue reading.

Because they are not established in the field of professional illustrating, most beginning illustrators have to search for stories to illustrate. That can take a lot of time. Out of necessity, I started writing my own stories. To my surprise, I soon discovered that I enjoyed writing as much as I liked to draw and paint. I found writing and illustrating to be natural partners.

Writers and illustrators do have much in common. Both are keen observers who analyze the environment around them and constantly study all aspects of human behavior, attitudes, and emotions. Both must also develop settings, characters, and the pace of a book. The only difference in their creative processes involves the tools each employs — the illustrator uses brushes and paint; the writer uses a typewriter or word processor.

Furthermore, there is no law that says a writer cannot become an illustrator, too, or that an illustrator cannot write stories. Many have successfully done both, such as Beatrix Potter, Dr. Seuss, Arnold Lobel, and Tomie dePaola. As a writer and illustrator myself, the combination fascinates me, and I firmly believe most artists have the ability to be good writers and many writers can become good illustrators.

In the *Written & Illustrated By . . .* workshops I conduct nationwide to teach students to create original books, I always insist that each participant write and illustrate his or her own book. The students who are artistically inclined moan and groan, and say they can't write. Others, who are more interested in writing, complain and say they can't "draw a straight line." But by the end of every workshop, the writers have developed wonderful illustrations and the artists have written exciting, often touching stories.

If you are a young person who wants to illustrate books, no matter what medium you wish to use — pen and ink, watercolor, tempera, or photography — I urge you to start writing too. It can help you expand your understanding and skills in the development of plot and characters. And whether or not you become a published author, the experiences you gain by writing stories will help you analyze and recognize the flow and content of good pieces of writing.

There are thousands of exceptionally talented young authors and illustrators who deserve to have their works published. To provide them with publishing opportunities, in association with Landmark Editions, Inc., I initiated *The National Written & Illustrated By . . . Awards Contest for Students.* Young people, ages six to nineteen, may participate in our annual contest. Each year Landmark publishes the winning students' books.

Many people believe that artists and writers have to be thirty or forty years old before their books can be published. But this is not true. To date, Landmark has published sixteen books by young authors and illustrators, including *World War Won*, by Dav Pilkey, age nineteen; *Elmer the Grump*, by Elizabeth Haidle, age fourteen; and *Strong and Free*, by Amy Hagstrom, age nine. And six-year-old Dennis Volmer, the author and illustrator of *Joshua Disobeys*, holds the record in the 1990 *Guinness Book of World Records* as the youngest author and illustrator of a published book.

I am delighted to say to young writers and illustrators nationwide — you no longer have to wait until you are ancient, or even an adult, to have your works published. Many opportunities are available now through a variety of sources, including Landmark's unique contest and educational programs, that encourages students to be creative.

More than 7,000 original books were received for the 1990 Landmark contest. So what are you waiting for? Start writing and illustrating your story today and enter it in the next contest! Perhaps you, too, will become the author and illustrator of a published book!

Deborah Valentine_____

Editor of "The Write Words" for *Youth View*

As a former teacher and frequent guest speaker in schools, Deborah Valentine has had a lot of opportunity to encourage creativity among students. As the editor of "The Write Words" column for Youth View, *a newsmagazine primarily for families in Georgia, she now also has the opportunity to share students' writing and art in a traditional publishing format. Those are opportunities that not only give her great pleasure but, she has found, also enhance her own creativity.*

Ms. Valentine is the founder of Valentine Productions, a company that produces and distributes audio and video tapes and books for children and their parents. In addition she is the author of the Educational Play series by Trillium Press and she has had over 500 news and feature articles published.

Illustrations sometimes tell more than words. As editor of "The Write Words" column for *Youth View* newsmagazine in Atlanta, Georgia, I sometimes run across poems or stories that I am undecided about. Should I include them? If the poem or story has a charming illustration with it, many times the answer will be yes.

I've always been a "visual" person. When I was growing up, I tended to choose books that included illustrations. Even now, I tend to learn better when I write things down or see an illustration of a concept. The illustrations I like best for the *Youth View* column include even more information or detail than the words of the story or poem. Like the wonderful books about Clifford, the big red dog, the illustrations sometimes carry the story forward, or help make a funny comment on an obvious understatement.

Many children believe they have to be good artists to illustrate a story. They believe that the children and bicycles and trees that they draw must look exactly like those things. These children should remember, if I wanted an exact picture of birds or swingsets, I would simply use a photograph. It is precisely because their drawings are not perfect that children's illustrations hold so much fascination for young people and adults alike.

Some children write a story and then draw a picture to go with it. However, I noticed in my twelve years of teaching that some children like to draw a picture first and then write a story or poem about it. If you are a visual learner the way I am, you may find than drawing the picture first helps give you ideas and helps you organize your thoughts as you write. A picture can be like a visual "outline" of your writing.

Drawing pictures to accompany stories or poems is a personal activity. Children are sharing themselves in their illustrations just as they are in their personal experience stories. Such sharing takes courage! I'm always proud of the children who send in their drawing along with their writing. I want to say, "Good work, keep it up." And the best way to say this is by publishing their pictures and stories. As a matter of fact, working with young illustrators and writers has stimulated my own writing. I'm grateful to have a job that helps me encourage creativity in youngsters.

Tracey Holloway_____
American Morgan Horse Association, Art
Contest Coordinator

*Though Tracey Holloway started out as an art
major in college, she later switched to political
science. But she's never lost her love for art
and enjoys coordinating the annual AMHA art
contest as part of her job as director of communications.*

*She was particularly impressed with the quality of art work entered in
the 1989 contest from young people in the fourteen- to seventeen-year-old
category. "They [the art works] were so competitive," she says. "And, as a
group, displayed among the most professional quality work." She points out
that the overall winner was also relatively young, a nineteen-year-old college
student who incorporated both historical and modern-day aspects of the
breed into her painting. Says Ms. Holloway, "It had ghosts of Morgans past,
as well as presenting the modern aspect."*

*Surprisingly, Ms. Holloway didn't start riding herself until age twenty-
four. She now owns her own horse, a gelding named Boca, and prefers
hunting and jumping.*

Many young people love horses but are not able to own one. The
American Morgan Horse Association (AMHA) Art and Photograph contests are held each year as another way to involve
young people with the Morgan breed. The contests also serve as a
fundraiser and as a way to obtain promotional material for the
AMHA. Many entries are sent in with the hope that the artwork
or photograph will one day be seen on the cover of the prestigious
breed journal, *The Morgan Horse*, as an illustration for an advertisement, as a photograph of the month in the AMHA Calendar,
or in the promotional literature designed to increase interest in the
Morgan horse.

When entering either contest it is important to follow all the
directions on the entry form. All art work must be matted or
framed. Some of the photographs are submitted matted or framed
but this is not a requirement. It is also very important to pack your

work carefully for shipping. When sending more than one photo, place a sheet of paper between the photos. This will insure that the photos arrive clean and in reproducible condition. Nothing is more heartbreaking than to open a box and discover a broken sculpture, crumpled artwork, or torn canvas.

The guidelines for the AMHA Art Contest state that work is judged on creativity, artistic quality, breed promotion, and overall appearance. This means you must be familiar with the subject before attempting to portray the Morgan horse in an artistic medium. AMHA is happy to provide you with colorful brochures of the Morgan breed and booklets that describe the breed standards. Your local public or school library may also be a good source of information on what a Morgan horse looks like, how they differ from other breeds of horses, their historical significance, and other general interest information. You may want to visit a Morgan farm near you for a firsthand look at a Morgan horse. Morgan owners are very friendly and love to share their animals with the public. Ask for a list of breeders and owners in your area when you contact the AMHA for an entry form.

The information about the Art Contest also applies to the AMHA Photo Contest, which is coordinated by Sally Wadhams, our director of youth and education. The photographs must depict the theme and include a registered Morgan horse. The 1990 theme was "Morgans, Just for the Fun of It." Entries are judged on creativity, spontaneity of subject, technical quality, breed promotion, and overall appearance.

I hope these are helpful tips on producing a winning piece for the AMHA Art and Photo Contests. Remember to follow the directions on the entry form, know your subject, pack your work carefully for shipping, and ask friends or family members to take a look at what you are planning to send. A well planned and carefully prepared entry shows seriousness and commitment – qualities the judges are looking for.

Cash awards and ribbons are given for both contests. If you enter a contest and want to know how your work was received, you may want to call the contest sponsors for feedback. This will help you with your future entries. The most important thing is to keep trying and to do your very best. This will produce winners every time.

Ellen S. Thomas_____

Young People's Film & Video Festival,
Coordinator

Though Ellen Thomas, Education Coordina-
tor for the Northwest Film & Video Center, has
a masters degree in film and once worked as a
free-lance film and video producer before as-
suming her present position, as a child she was never exposed to the wide
variety of opportunities in film production. It just wasn't a topic commonly
explored in the small Iowa town where she grew up. Her initial interest in
film came from still photography, a hobby she still enjoys.

In addition to overseeing the annual Festival competition, which draws
between sixty and seventy-five entries each year, Ms. Thomas coordinates a
state-wide artist-in-residence program and a continuing education curricu-
lum of classes and visiting artist seminars. She points out that while the
Festival is restricted to students from Oregon, Washington, Idaho, Montana,
and Alaska, similar projects do exist in other areas. And where there is no
current project, a local or state art council might be persuaded to start one
provided there is enough interest and support. The Northwest Film & Video
Center is a division of the Oregon Art Institute.

As television viewers and movie-goers, most young people are on
the receiving end of film and videomaking rather than the sending
end, especially since studies show that the average teenager watches
five or more hours of television per day. As a result, one common
misconception that aspiring young film or videomakers often have
is that film or videomaking is *easy.* Just aim the camcorder and
shoot, and the camera will take care of everything.

But as anyone who has planned and produced a film or video
production, especially an award-winning one, will tell you, nothing
could be further from the truth. A two hour Hollywood movie may
take as long as sixteen weeks to shoot, even with a crew of sixty
highly trained people working fourteen hours a day, six days a
week. And that's just the filming part of the work! Editing, or "post
production," can easily take another six months.

Another mistaken assumption is that one person (such as the

director) can be totally responsible for what a completed piece looks, sounds, and feels like. Filmmaking is collaborative. One person cannot run all of the equipment and supervise all of the action at the same time. Rarely are the multiple talents and abilities required in the filmmaking process (including photography, research, music composition, dramatic writing, graphic arts, set design, and acting) present in one person. A team is required, even though one coach or star may be the guiding force behind the group effort.

But what distinguishes filmmaking from other team activities, of course, is the fact that it is an art form. It has what is called a "language." Camera angles, camera movement, packing, coloration, and many other factors work together to create an intentional mood and message — its individual *language*. Like writers and dramatists, filmmakers use this language to tell a story and convey values that they believe are important. Every film, whether a serious documentary, animated comedy, or personal philosophical exploration, offers an opinion about the world in the way it chooses to portray people, their problems, and the way problems are resolved. Like a good professional filmmaker, the beginner will need to employ a good deal of creativity and persistence in locating and utilizing the appropriate language for the piece being captured.

Given these challenges, where does a young person interested in film or videomaking begin? And what kinds of work receive recognition in film competitions like the Northwest Film & Video Center's *Young Peoples' Film & Video Festival?*

Many award-winning entries in our Festival have been produced as school projects with the class as a whole being recognized as the "winner." Many of them received outside artistic assistance, some in the form of an "artist-in-residence" program. Using limited professional help is not discouraged by the Festival. The important things are that the subject and approach of the finished production represent the creativity, hard work, and collaboration of the students involved.

Every entry, regardless of the applicant, is judged according to its clarity (does it make its point without overdoing or underdoing it?); freshness (has it been done before?); originality (imprint your own style); appropriateness (is it a work that exemplifies excellence on the part of young filmmakers?); and aesthetic style (does the "language" used convey the subject in a meaningful way?).

Specifically, while you are making your film or video production, keep this in mind: Filmmaking is repetitive. Write your script and then re-write it − it can always be better. Pre-plan, re-plan, and then plan some more. Rehearse it and then re-rehearse it. Shoot it and then re-shoot the part that aren't as good as you want them to be. (These are called "pick-ups.")

The same applies to editing: When you have finished editing, have an outsider look at it. It can probably be shorter. Length is not an official criteria but it can have a subconscious effect on the jurors. In film and video contests around the country, professional and amateur, short pieces always outnumber long pieces as winners, probably because a well-edited film makes its point without unnecessary footage.

Estimate the amount of production time you believe will be needed and then multiply that by *three* to find out what really will be required. It is not important that your work looks "professional" but employ your technical know-how throughout. For instance, prevent shadows by using lights. Avoid a hollowed-out voice track by using an external microphone. Add music, your own original music if possible. In using special effects, apply them sparingly and in a meaningful way − not just for the sake of including them. The extra work you invest will be readily apparent in the final product. Winners are very hard workers.

Take pride in your effort. Put titles at the beginning and end (even if you just shoot a hand-lettered tagboard) and thank everyone involved, including your funders, of course, as well as the people who helped you along the way. Send a good quality duplicate copy with the entry form (never let the master out of your possession) and label it clearly with the title and applicant name. Last, have fun with the project and don't be afraid to let it show. Film and videomaking are, after all, entertainment. And before long, if you are bitten with the filmmaking bug, you will probably start another film project. Might as well enjoy yourself along the way.

Richard M. Myers

Biology Teacher, Portland Public Schools, Oregon

Richard M. Myers is proof that students can benefit by incorporating creative writing and visual art projects into the school curriculum. As a biology teacher in the Portland, Oregon public school system, he has encouraged student participation in producing films as part of his advanced biology program.

The class, he says, provides students with access to professional biologists and involvement with scientific problems and issues. This unique approach has allowed students to participate in the development of original curriculum materials of national significance, including award-winning documentary films. Mr. Myers points out that with adult help, students who have a variety of skills and talents can participate in similar projects.

In 1988, Mr. Myers' Cleveland High School advanced biology class won top honors at the Young Peoples' Film & Video Festival. Here he explains how the twenty-three minute film, "The Columbia River Gorge: A Natural History," project was organized and carried out. As the supervising adult for the project, he works with his students in much the same way as an editor or art director would.

In our project, the Experiential Biology class was able to investigate local natural history and ecology topics while integrating students' skills in script writing, composition and production of an original musical score, speaking in the narration, applying visual skills in cinematography — all the while studying biology.

Through the area "Artist-in-the-Schools Program," I arranged for outside help, particularly with the filmmaking portion of the project, a situation that the Festival organizers encourage. By having a professional filmmaker available, students were able to experience firsthand how their contributions could be integrated into the final production.

With the resources of the filmmaker available, the class was able to set out to make a biology film of their own choice. In less than a year, the project produced a twenty-three minute documentary color film on the natural history of the Columbia River Gorge. In addition to receiving much recognition, the film has been viewed by many audiences, including a special showing at the Smithsonian's National Museum of Natural History in Washington, DC. The film is now a resource in many educational film libraries and continues to receive many requests for showing. There is also a study guide to be used with the film.

Participation in this project allowed students the opportunity to study the environment of the Pacific Northwest in a unique manner. Not only did they have to investigate the natural history in great detail, but they had to compile this information into a script that would make possible a production to be shared with a diverse audience. The students had to research scientific literature, interview practicing biologists, and find suitable sites for recording this information as a visual image. Under the guidance of the artists-in-residence, the students worked on script writing, camera operation, and filming; wrote original music for the score; constructed clay models for clay animation sequences; and suggested many ideas about the message the film should carry.

The result is a product that describes a special environment of incredible intrinsic value. Audiences who view the film are rewarded with an enjoyable experience and a greater understanding of the magnificence of the natural world.

Since then, new students have produced two additional documentaries. *Forest in the City* is a seventeen minute film about Forest Park located in Portland, Oregon. *Cascade Watershed* is a twenty-one minute film about the Sandy River Basin.

Mercedes A. Quiroga

Director of Adjudication, Arts Recognition
and Talent Search

Mercedes Quiroga knows exactly when she first became interested in the arts. She was twelve years old when she accompanied her mother on a trip to New York City. Once there an older cousin took her to see a performance of Swan Lake by the American Ballet Theater. "She also took me to see a play and to a couple of museums," says Ms. Quiroga. "And ever since I've been hooked on the arts, especially the visual arts."

She earned a major in art history from the University of Miami (Florida), and began working with the ARTS program after first serving as a "collection communicator" at a Miami-Dade museum that specialized in displaying decorative and propaganda arts. A hobby photographer, she prefers to shoot black and white film with her Pentax cameras, then develop the prints herself.

Arts Recognition and Talent Search (ARTS) is a unique program that recognizes the achievements of high school seniors and other seventeen- and eighteen-year-old artists in all art areas: dance, music, theater, writing, and visual arts, including film and video.

Each year ARTS reviews over 5000 total applications with approximately 1000 entries in the visual arts category alone. Applicants in the area of visual arts are required to submit slides or videos, depending on their medium, to illustrate the quality of their work. The application process is quite rigorous and is often the first time young artists are introduced to the mechanisms of presentation and critical evaluations.

The ARTS award candidates selected for final adjudication [judging] are convened in Miami annually during the second week of January, at the program's expense. Here, each artist is evaluated through a series of interviews and offered counseling, advanced training, and enrichment workshops with prominent, nationally known artists and educators. Based on the judges' evaluations,

ARTS award candidates can receive unrestricted cash awards ranging from $500 to $3,000.

In addition to this, the ARTS program is the vehicle by which high school students are nominated to become Presidential Scholars in the Arts, the highest honor for high school seniors. Winners are invited to several days of events and ceremonies in Washington, DC, culminating in a White House reception with the President.

The preparation is challenging but the rewards are many as the ARTS program is nationally recognized as one of the largest private sources of financial aid and grants available for artistically gifted high school students. ARTS is funded by the National Foundation for Advancement in the Arts and is administered by Miami-Dade Community College, Wolfson Campus.

The application process is two-fold. First, you submit an application along with a small fee, which the ARTS office processes and in turn sends you an Application Packet. Second, you must read over the material contained in the Application Packet and follow all instructions carefully in order to submit your slides or video as indicated. Our office will be glad to answer any questions pertaining to this process. Please call us at (305) 347-3416, and if you leave a message on our "phonemail" we will return your call, or you may write us at ARTS, 300 N.E. 2 Avenue, Miami, FL 33132.

Larry W. Wood_____

Computer Art & Graphics Forums,
Administrator

*Larry Wood is a self-taught computer enthusi-
ast who currently serves as the administrator
of several electronic forums and other information products available on-line through the
CompuServe Information Service (CIS).*

*While researching tourist information for computer buffs who were
planning visits to the central Florida area, he met and became friends with a
twelve-year-old boy from Jacksonville, Florida, who suggested that computer
graphics, such as pictures, would be a good addition to the available information. Out of that friendship and idea has grown the world's largest collection of on-line graphics.*

For many years, we, as a society, have been told that computers are
the way of the future; that they would become as commonplace in
the home as the TV. The youth of today find it hard to imagine a
school without computers, while not many years ago (at least not
THAT many years ago) during my own childhood, calculators were
not even available. What a wonderful world we live in, where what
the future holds for us is limited only by the imagination of our
children.

Having purchased my first computer (at age thirty-nine), I was
immediately intimidated by the vastness of what I had to learn in
order to compete with those around me, all of whom seemed to
know everything there was to know about computers. The most
knowledgeable were the young people, who seemed to have mas-
tered this mysterious world of bytes bits, disks, programs, and utili-
ties. It was embarrassing to walk into the local Radio Shack store
to ask a beginner's question, while the twelve or thirteen year old
next to me was discussing mathematical co-processors.

What I needed was a one-stop source of information in an environment where no one would recognize me. That environment
became obvious when I found a subscription to CompuServe, the

world's largest information service. Hooking my computer up to a modem and hesitantly dialing into the network for the first time changed my life forever. Space, auto racing, encyclopedia services, computer hard/software, and so many other information sources became immediately available. What a wonderful world of information I had found. Computing from place to place on the network became an adventure, an awesome, exciting adventure.

Soon after discovering the world of on-line computing, I approached CompuServe with the idea of providing on-line tourist information about the central Florida area. *Discover Orlando* was born, with *The Florida Forum* quickly following. While hosting a live, on-line computer conference from Coco Beach, Florida one evening, I was approached by a twelve-year-old boy, who asked why we couldn't provide pictures of Disney World, Sea World, and Kennedy Space Center over the computer. That question started several members of CompuServe thinking and the idea of providing photographs in computer graphics format developed into what is now the world's largest collection of on-line computer graphics. We attribute our success today to that twelve-year-old boy, who was not afraid to ask a question.

Providing answers to beginning computer enthusiasts is what we do best in the forums. Our philosophy, along with the laid-back, easy-going question and answer format of *The Graphics Forums*, provides a perfect environment for young people to learn how to use their computers as effective tools in the graphics arena, as well as providing a huge source of computer graphics for their on- and off-line viewing pleasure.

The various graphics forums also provide a gallery-style showcase for young artists. They can upload their artwork to the forums and thousands of other forum members can then download and view the product of their efforts. Artwork can be created on or by the computer, or in other more traditional mediums and, through the use of scanners, digitizers, and capture boards, be converted to computer graphics format. Young artists are encouraged to submit their artwork and participate in the forum's Hall of Fame Contests. Other contests and projects, specifically geared to young people, are being developed.

Mike Wilmer_____
Photography Forum and Contest,
Administrator

A professional photographer who frequently criss-crosses the United States on assignment, Mike Wilmer wouldn't be able to pursue his business-related hobby if it weren't for a travel-size computer (more commonly known as a "laptop") and a modem. That equipment allows him to communicate to members of his Photography Forum *whenever and from wherever he happens to be, as long as he can connect to a phone line. In fact, except for the picture above, Mr. Wilmer submitted all the material for this profile through forum messages and library files, or the electronic mail services on CompuServe. (Note: the receiving editor also had to have the necessary equipment and access to CompuServe in order to receive the information on-line.)*

Someday, when he retires, he hopes to open a photo gallery where people can come and view examples of his work. In the meantime, however, he offers CompuServe users an opportunity to display their photography through various forum libraries as well as through the Photography Forum's *annual contest.*

The *Photography Forum* contests are skill-based and open to regular customers, over twelve years of age, of the CompuServe Information Service. There are two divisions, one for professionals and the other for amateur photographers. If you earn more than 50% of your income from photography, you are considered a professional, for the purposes of this contest. Prizes vary each year depending on who that year's sponsors are. For instance, in 1990, Vivitar, Fuji, and Camera One contributed prizes that included two gold zoom lenses packaged in velvet-lined boxes (commemorating Vivitar's 50th Anniversary) and assortments of Fuji film. In addition, first and second place winners received a free month's access to the *Photography Forum*. Winning photos are also sometimes published in *CompuServe Magazine*.

The object of the contest is to create a photograph suitable for conversion to "GIF," CompuServe's Graphic Interchange Format.

Obviously, the photographs making the greatest impact as graphic images win. Therefore, entrants should remember that simple images have more potential to win than complex images. That's because subtle detail in a "busy" photograph will be lost in a graphic conversion, so images with very distinct lines are preferred. For example, a close-up of a daisy will *digitize* better than a field of daisies.

Contest photographs may be uploaded directly to the *Photography Forum* if you know how to convert them into GIF format yourself, or have someone who knows how that can help you. If you want additional help in creating GIF images, you can leave a message to the sysop or check out the information available in the *Graphics Support Forum* also on CompuServe. Whether you upload a graphic image of your photograph or not, you must also send a copy to the *Photography Forum* by regular U.S. mail. The address can be found in each year's contest rules, which are always available in a special forum library file. Photographs will *not* be returned, so be sure to send a copy and keep the original.

A two-tier judging system determines the photographs best suited for conversion to GIF. Then those selected will be converted to GIF, if they haven't already been uploaded in that format, and displayed in the *Photography Forum*. Semi-finalists are judged by interested forum members and forum sysops, with voting done by private message. Forum members who are interested in judging can apply for a week of free access to the *Photography Forum*. The first four applicants with the necessary hardware (having the capability to view graphic images in GIF format on your personal computer monitor) will be accepted.

The way we judge our photography contests, by digitizing the finalist entries, makes them unique because it allows our judges, who are located all over the country, to view entries on their own computers before making their selections of the best. Since digital imaging is going to become a major force in the photographic industry in the future, that slant to our contest is terribly important.

One additional point: members of the *Photography Forum* are extremely willing to welcome young people into the forum. Whether it's a company representative, a writer for a photo publication, or a professional in the field, they're all quick to lend a helping hand, giving the newcomer the benefit of their experience. I only wish I had had access to so many knowledgeable people when I was starting out. When you think about it, the "consultation" fee is pretty reasonable. <smile>

CHAPTER FOUR

How to Prepare Your Work for Submission

Next to the care and attention you put into creating your work, nothing is more important than the care you take in presenting it to an editor or a contest judge. Damage caused by careless handling, storage, or mailing can turn a photo or artwork worthy of publication into one that will prompt a quick rejection note.

Important also, if you want your work seriously considered, is the medium you choose to work with and the form you mail it in. There are some contests, such as the ones sponsored by the American Morgan Horse Association, where you can submit work in almost *any* medium. For example, you could use crayons, acrylic or oil paints, modeling clay, or scrap iron to make your entry. And you can use either, or *both*, black and white or color film to take photographs. Plus, your entry may be a realistic representation or pure whimsy or fantasy, just as long as you incorporate a Morgan horse in your design. Your art entry, if it's a painting or illustration, must be matted before sending; however, your photos do not. The entry form may be one supplied by AMHA or a photocopy of one someone has.

Other markets and contests, on the other hand, are very specific regarding what material you may use to create your piece *and* the way you mail it. For example, to enter the annual "Traffic Safety Poster" program sponsored by the American Automobile Association (AAA) you *must* mail your poster *flat*. You are not permitted to send it rolled up in a tube. Also, your entry must be related to *only* one of the two slogans assigned to your state and grade classification. While you may reword the slogan as long as the slogan's message is not changed, you *may not* invent your own slogan.

Other markets or contests may insist that only an official entry form can be used, and some have no entry forms at all. Because of production requirements, many magazine, newsletter, and newspaper markets will only consider line drawings done in black and white or photos in black and white.

It is extremely important that you follow the specific guidelines requested by a particular market or contest when submitting your work. Otherwise, your work will be rejected no matter how good it may be. Worse, some markets and contests won't return an inappropriate submission even if accompanied by a SASE. And *no* market will assume responsibility for unsolicited artwork or photographs.

With so many variations in policy, it's impossible to give specific advice for preparing all types of artwork and photos in this Guide. What follows are the general guidelines and formats that most magazines and contests will accept. (Note: The standard format for manuscripts is more uniform. Detailed information can be found in *Market Guide for Young Writers.* Some of the basic guidelines are included here where appropriate.)

Model Release Forms

Occasionally a publication or contest will ask that the artist, photographer, or author provide a statement signed by the person granting an interview or allowing photograph to be taken, in order to prove that he or she agreed to being interviewed or photographed, and that the person realizes how the material might be used (such as in a magazine). When the person signs the form it means that he is saying that it's okay to publish the material. Such a form is known as a "model release." Sometimes a market will supply a copy of the model release form they prefer, or you can find examples of them in reference books. (See Appendix Two.) However, if only a simple form is needed you can make one up yourself. Here's how:

Using a clean sheet of paper write your name, address, phone number, and the name, address, phone number of the person being interviewed, photographed, or used as a model. Have that person write a sentence or two that clearly shows he or she understands that the information or photograph, etc., may be published or used for publicity purposes. You could write up this statement ahead of time. Then have the person sign his or her name and that day's date. You would also sign the form. If possible, have another person sign it too, as a witness. If you are dealing with someone eighteen or younger, have a parent or guardian also sign the model release form.

Note that you do not need to provide this form unless the market or contest specifically requests it. But since you may not always know when you'll need to send one, it's a good idea to have a model release form signed by anyone readily identifiable in a photograph you hope to have published.

Artwork

While some larger, flexible pieces of artwork, such as posters and illustrations may be rolled up and sent in a special cardboard mailing tube, most markets and contests prefer that artwork be mailed *flat*. You especially don't want to fold or crease it in anyway.

Protect the surface of your art with a sheet of paper so that it doesn't become smudged or dirtied. To mail it, put your artwork between two pieces of sturdy cardboard cut slightly larger than the artwork itself. Secure with at least two rubberbands. Ordinary manila folders, large enough to hold your work, cardboard, and extra papers such as entry forms or a manuscript, may be used to mail your entry. For pieces larger than 9" X 12", it's best to use a shipping envelope that has a special lining made of plastic bubbles or other filling. These may be found at art and office supply stores. They may also be carried in your local grocery or department store. For overly-large artwork, you may need to make your own mailing "envelope" by measuring and cutting sheets of sturdy cardboard from a box (such as the ones televisions, bikes, or other things come in). Be sure to use strong, waterproof shipping tape on every exposed seam, as well as around the entire package, to ensure that it does not come open in transit.

Be sure to include your name, address, and phone somewhere on your artwork. (You'd be surprised at the number of artists and writers who forget!) Check the market or contest guidelines sheets for the specific location to put this information. Some like it on the back as long as it doesn't "bleed" through or otherwise damage the front of the picture. Often there is a small corner where you can put the information so that it doesn't interfere with the subject of the piece. Understand that this information is *in addition to* any personal signature that you include directly in your illustration or painting.

Some contests do not want personal information to appear on the artwork itself. In this case, be sure you have included the proper entry form with all the necessary information.

Self-Addressed Stamped Envelopes

Whether you are sending pictures, photographs, or a manuscript, most contests and markets expect you to include a self-addressed stamped envelope (SASE) with your submission. In fact, many will not even consider your submission without one. You should also include a SASE any time you write to any editor, contest sponsor, or other person and you would like a personal reply. The person will use this envelope to return your manuscript to you if he decides not to accept it, or to send the material you have requested.

When addressing your mailing envelope, use the editor's name whenever possible. Such as:

```
Susie Kaufmann                                          Place
2151 Hale Rd.                                           Stamp
Sandusky, MI 48471                                      Here


  ↑              Stone Soup
4⅛"              Gerry Mandel, Editor
  ↓              Children's Art Foundation
                 P.O. Box 83
                 Santa Cruz, CA 95063



                  ← 9½" →
```

Figure 1. Sample Mailing Envelope

You can locate the name of the current editor by checking the masthead, usually located near the front of the publication.

Use a second envelope for your self-addressed stamped envelope (SASE). Fold it in half to fit in the mailing envelope. Make sure your return envelope is large enough to hold your artwork without damaging it, and that it contains enough postage to cover the return trip. (That means if it costs you $1.25 to mail your manuscript and illustrations, put $1.25 worth of postage on your SASE.)

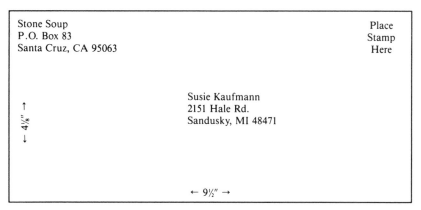

Figure 2. Sample SASE

An editor will not return your material if you forget to enclose a self-addressed stamped envelope with the right amount of postage. Some editors will not even read a manuscript or consider artwork and photographs that are not accompanied by a SASE. This may not seem like a good way to do business, but editors cannot afford to pay for the return of materials from every person who submits material. It would cost them thousands of dollars each year! They would rather use the money to pay writers for work that is accepted for publication.

A few of the markets and contests state they do not return material at all. You do not need to include a self-addressed stamped envelope with your material when submitting artwork to these markets and contests.

If you are worried that your package may not reach an editor, or if you want to make sure your package did arrive at a market that will not send it back, you may enclose a special self-addressed stamped postcard. (See Figures 3 and 4.) Most editors will take the time to mark a postcard and return it to you.

Always make a copy of your artwork, and have extra prints of photographs, when submitting to a market that will return your work, and *especially* to those that won't. It is insurance against a package that is damaged or lost in the mail. Occasionally, an editor will want to discuss your work with you over the phone. It is much easier when you both have a copy to look at. While making a copy of artwork is not always possible, and not always easy when it is possible, try to keep *some* type of copy for your records. This might be a photocopy or photograph of your artwork. In the case of regular photographs, your negative can serve as your copy. However, you may want to have duplicate prints (especially of slides) made if you want to be sure of having a duplicate. Copies of manuscripts can be made by using carbon paper, retyping a piece, using a photo-copying machine, or storing a copy on a computer disk.

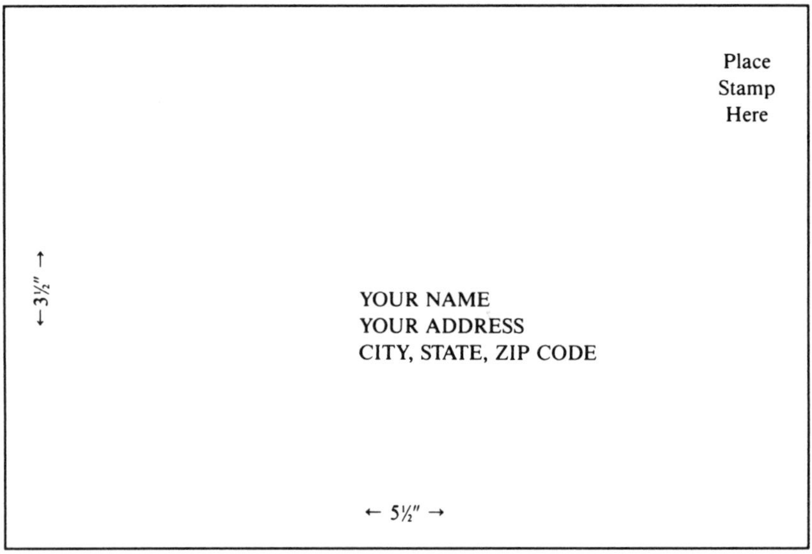

Place
Stamp
Here

↑
—3½″—
↓

YOUR NAME
YOUR ADDRESS
CITY, STATE, ZIP CODE

← 5½″ →

Figure 3. Front of Postcard

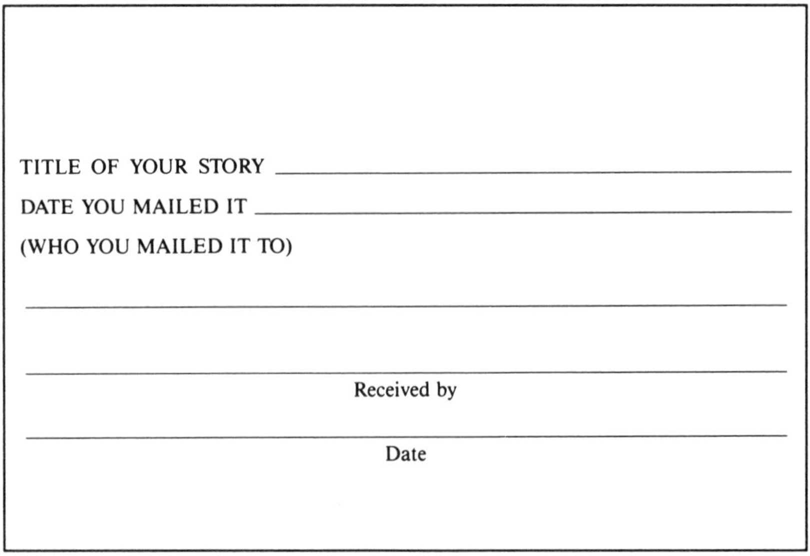

TITLE OF YOUR STORY _____

DATE YOU MAILED IT _____

(WHO YOU MAILED IT TO)

_____

_____
Received by

_____
Date

Figure 4. Message Side of Postcard

Dummy Books

If you like to both write and draw or take photographs, you may want to submit a book project to a book editor or special contest like the ones sponsored by Landmark Editions or Raintree Publishers. Professional writers and artists often include what is known as a "dummy" with their typed manuscript and a few pertinent examples of their art or photography. While it's unusual for young artists and photographers to include a dummy with their submission, you might like to make one up anyway. A dummy helps a person visualize the completed project with all the text and pictures roughly in place.

To make a dummy, fold several sheets of paper to form a "book," keeping in mind that the number of pages in a book is usually in multiples of eight or sixteen. For instance, most picture books are thirty-two or forty-eight pages long. That includes not only the story but several pages in the front of the book (front matter) for a title page, copyright page, table of contents, etc., plus "back matter" where a short biography of the author is usually located. Back matter also includes the glossary, index, bibliography, and appendices when appropriate.

Your dummy book doesn't need to be the same size as what you expect the finished book to be. In fact, dummies are almost always smaller because they often contain what are known as "thumbnail" sketches, rather than the full art. Therefore, one standard sheet of 8½" X 11" or 11" X 14" of typing or drawing paper can easily be folded to make an eight-page book. Use two sheets folded together to make a sixteen-page book.

What you include in your dummy often depends on whether you are more artist/photographer or writer. Writers sometimes print the entire text by placing parts of it on appropriate pages or by typing the story on a sheet of paper that they then cut up and paste in the book. The "illustrations" that a writer adds might just be squiggles indicating where pictures should go. These squiggles might even be simple drawings. Artists, on the other hand, especially those who also like to write, include not only the text (spaced appropriately throughout the book) but more detailed illustrations.

A major benefit of creating a dummy is that it helps the writer or artist see exactly how much text and/or illustrations or photos are needed. You will be able to easily tell if your story is too long for a standard-size book. Artists will be able to tell not only how many pictures they need to draw but of what size (depending on the part of the story that is being depicted) and what kind — for instance a small half or quarter page illustration or a large, double page spread such as the one in Maurice Sendak's famous book, *Where the Wild Things Are.*

In addition to creating their own dummies, writers and artists interested in creating picture books should study the many beautiful ones that have already been published to get a feel for how the text and illustrations work together to make the book a whole. Picture books are a good example of the adage that says the sum of two parts sometimes exceeds the whole. A good story combined with the right illustrations makes a single book that is far better than either the story or illustrations alone.

If you decide to both write and draw your own book, be sure to submit the text portion in the proper manuscript format, which is given later in this chapter.

Photographs

Some markets and contests insist, and most prefer, that you shoot with 35mm film at the lowest shutter speed possible that will still give you a clean, unblurred image. According to a survey done by professional photographer Lawrence F. Abrams, editors with a preference like photographers to use Kodak film. However, the majority did not indicate a preference. What was most important was the quality of the photo.

In the same survey, 95% of the editors said they preferred that photos unmounted (or unmatted) be submitted. However, you should always protect your photos by putting them between two pieces of sturdy cardboard, then wrapping the cardboard with two rubberbands. If you are sending more than one photograph, separate them with tissue paper or other paper that won't scratch the surface of the print. Except in rare instances, you would *never* send a negative. Avoid paperclipping a photo (or any artwork) to a sheet of paper or thin sheet of cardboard because the clip will almost always bend or dent the picture.

Slides, sometimes called transparencies, should be inserted in the pockets of a clear plastic slide holder sheet, available where most camera and film supplies are sold. Use this method also to protect slides you keep for yourself if they are important to you. However, avoid sheets made with plastic containing polyvinylchloride (PVC) if you expect your slides to be stored for a long time.

Be sure to identify every photo and slide you send. Most of the time you'll want to do this directly on the back of photos or on the sides of slides. A grease pencil, available at art or office supply stores, works well for writing on the back of photos without damaging them. Self-sticking name or address labels also will work. To avoid damaging the photo, *do not* write directly on the back with a pen or lead pencil.

You can safely write on the cardboard sides of slides, though some photographers type up small strips of self-sticking paper with their name and address. Many professionals have an inexpensive rubber stamp made with their name, address, and copyright notice on it, plus blank lines to write other identifying information about the slide.

Unless you are just sending a portrait-type photograph of yourself or someone else (often called a "head-shot"), you should always provide a caption for your photo that identifies the people in it and what is taking place. Sometimes you'll have room for this information to be placed directly on the back of each photo. However, it's best to also include a sheet with your submission that lists all the captions in one place. Be sure to number or code each photo or slide so it's easy to tell which caption goes with what photo.

Many times photos and slides may be submitted directly with a manuscript. There are some markets, however, that only want you to send these after the editor has requested them.

To help ensure that they get at least one good photograph or slide, many photographers "bracket" their pictures by taking several shots at different settings. This is a good practice for any photographer. However, don't send a whole batch of photographs to an editor or contest expecting someone to select the best ones. That's *your* job. When selecting which ones to choose, look for clear, clean pictures with good contrast and interesting content. Most times, an "action" shot is preferred to a photograph where everyone is staring into the camera. Also make sure that the subject of your photo takes up most of the frame. That is, don't send a photo of someone riding a bicycle where the rider and bike are just specks in the distance. And try to avoid chopping people's arms, legs, wrists, and ankles off at their joints. If you don't know what makes one photograph better than another, consult some of the resources listed in Appendix Two. As with writing and art, a good photographer improves with practice.

Three Dimensional Art

To mail three dimensional art, such as sculptures and models, choose a sturdy container. Heavy, corrugated cardboard boxes work well. Make sure that it isn't so big that your piece will tumble about, or so small that you can't insert adequate stuffing material. Try to insert the bottom of the piece into a foam liner or Styrofoam™ form that will hold it secure. Use additional foam, wadded newspaper, shipping "popcorn" (or real popcorn if the piece is lightweight), or sheets of plastic bubble material. These materials can be found at most office supply stores or you can save them from other packages that have come to your home or school. You might also be able to get free boxes and packing materials from a local appliance or furniture dealer.

Follow the guidelines to determine how the piece should be identified. And *always* include a slip of paper with your name, address, and phone *inside* the box in case the mailing label is lost or damaged. To protect your investment, send your art by registered mail or United Parcel Service. For markets and contests that will return unaccepted work and also accepted work after publication or display, enclose a SASE with instructions on how to mail it back to you. Rather than send return postage with your submission, you might prefer to have the editor or contest use your SASE (containing first class letter-size postage) to inform you first. Then you can send a check, supply the correct postage, or arrange for pickup by a courier service such as United Parcel. Whether or not you insure your artwork when mailing will be up to you. Ask for advice and information at the postal office or courier pick-up location.

Be aware that many contests, such as the ARTS Talent Search and many juried art shows and contests, as well as some markets, do not want you to send your original art pieces. For these, you will need to take slide pictures or regular photographs (depending on the market or contest). Since judges and editors can only make their selections from what they see in a slide or photograph, be sure to shoot them using the same attention to detail with which you created your piece in the first place. For advice on photographing your artwork (paintings as well as three dimensional pieces) see the resources in Appendix Two.

Manuscripts

While handwritten manuscripts by children fourteen and under are sometimes allowed by markets and contests, many prefer (and some *insist*) that manuscripts be typed. Whether you handwrite or type, there are some specific things to keep in mind.

Write or type on only one side of a sheet of paper. Leave ample margins of approximately 1½" on all four sides of each sheet. Put your name, address, phone number, and Social Security number or date of birth on the first sheet (except where contest rules differ). Then on each additional sheet, put your last name at the top left-hand corner, center a key word from your title on the same line, and place the page number at the far right side of the line.

Except for poetry, all manuscripts should be double-spaced. If you handwrite your manuscript, use lined paper and write on every other line, especially if you write big or use narrow-ruled paper. For typewritten work, use a nonerasable bond. (Sixteen- or twenty-pound weight is best.) For handwritten work, tablet or loose- leaf paper is acceptable. Don't tear pages from a spiral bound notebook because the ragged edges are a real nuisance to editors.

Pay attention to word length limits on fiction and nonfiction, and to line limits on poetry. If you include a manuscript with illustrations, try to include a second copy of the manuscript text prepared in the standard format. Remember to include SASE with your submission when appropriate.

your name,
address,
phone →
Soc. Security
number here

Susie Kaufmann
2151 Hale Rd.
Sandusky, MI 48471
(313) 555-2076
SS# 000-00-0000

About 800 words ← *word count*
Oct. 25, 1990 ← *date*

THE STOLEN TEST ← *title*
by
Susie Kaufmann ← *author*

Start your
story here →

Karen Mathis hurried down the deserted hall of Mayville
Junior High. She was late. There would be no time to study
before supper now.

"Darn," she grumbled. She was annoyed with herself for
leaving her history book in the gym. She had walked nearly
half way home before remembering it.

The empty building echoed with an eerie, hollow sound
like a cave along the seashore. Somewhere, a janitor
whistled "Yankee Doodle" as he slushed a pail of water
down a drain.

A door creaked behind her. Karen spun around. Her armload
of books slipped. She caught them before they fell.

"It's okay, Bud," someone whispered. "It's just Karen."

Travis Piper and Bud Watson slipped quietly out of

Figure 5. Sample Manuscript First Page

last name ↘

key word from title ↓

page number ↓

Kaufmann   STOLEN TEST   2

Mrs. Taylor's history room. "Let's get out of here,"

Travis whispered. He grabbed Karen by the arm and

rushed her toward the door.

    "Wait a minute," Karen objected. "What's going on?"

    "Shut-up," Travis ordered. "We'll fill you in outside."

    The three hurried out of the building. The sun was

beginning to settle behind the closely knit suburban

homes. Travis's firm grip of Karen's arm hurt. She

struggled to break loose.

Figure 6. Sample Manuscript Second Page

Keeping Track of Submissions

Once you decide to submit material to an editor or contest, you must also devise a system of keeping track of your work. This is especially important if you are anxious to get published and will be sending more than one piece of artwork or photographs and/or manuscripts out at the same time.

One way to keep track is with 3" X 5" index cards kept in a file box. Prepare a new index card for each work you send out. Along the top of each card write these headings:

	DATE	DATE
TITLE	MAILED	RETURNED
	MARKET	NOTES

↑ 3" ↓

← 5" →

Figure 7. Sample File Card

Record the title of your submission or contest entry, the date you mailed it (not the date you created it), and the name of the market or contest to which you sent it. Under "Notes" you may want to write down the amount of postage it cost to mail the package. Include the cost of the self-addressed stamped envelope and/or postcard too.

When you receive an answer from the editor or contest, write the date under the "Date Returned" heading. Under "Notes" or on the back of the card, mark whether the work was accepted or rejected and any other pertinent information, such as how much you were (or will be) paid for the piece and when the editor plans to publish it.

If the work was rejected, select another market from the lists. Mark the new information on the same card if there is room.

If students will be submitting material as part of a class project, one file box may be used to keep an accurate record of all student submissions and editors' remarks.

Similar records may also be kept in an extra notebook or in a file on a computer disk.

Additional Tips

Think ahead! If you're really anxious to submit material, don't wait until you have a work in completed form before sending away for market guidelines, sample copies, and detailed contest information. But don't send away for all of them at once either. Choose a few markets and contests that are looking for material similar to what you are most interested in producing. Consider also markets and contests directed especially toward young people your age.

Once the market and contest information begins arriving, you'll want an easy way to store it, so that when you have a work ready to submit, you can consult your market information and choose where you would like to send it first.

All this information can be kept in a desk drawer, a file cabinet, or even a shoe box. An even better method is to make your own personal marketing guide. You'll need a large three ring binder and a box of vinyl sheet protectors. Top-loading sheet protectors work best. You might also want a package of tab dividers to separate various types of markets and contests, or to file information alphabetically.

When a sample copy and guideline sheet arrive, slip them into a sheet protector for safe keeping. Some sample copies won't fit into the sheet protector. You'll have to store these somewhere else. Put a note on the corresponding guideline sheet to remind yourself where the sample copy is. Insert a reference sheet at the front of your binder to record which market and contest information you have. Also include the date you received the information and the date of the sample copy so you'll know when you need to send for more current information.

Your personal marketing guide is also an excellent place to keep additional notes or how-to articles about drawing, painting, shooting pictures, writing, etc.; the names and addresses of new markets and contests; samples of published material you think is well done; and even your record of submissions. If you attend young author/artist conferences and creativity workshops, or have professional artists, photographers, or authors speak to your class, store your notes or any handout material in your marketing guide for easy reference.

CHAPTER FIVE
Understanding a Market Listing

Markets, which include secular and religious magazines, newspapers, newsletters, book publishers, and other sources, are arranged alphabetically for easy reference. Markets that are accessed by modem through on-line computer services are listed together in Chapter Nine.

Each listing contains three individual sections of information that will help you understand: (1) the type of market it is, (2) what material it will consider from young people, and (3) how to submit your work. There are two optional sections. "Editor's Remarks" are quotes directly from editors or their guideline sheets. They provide additional information to help you submit your material to the appropriate market. The "Subscription Rates" section has been included as an extra service since so many of the publications listed are available by subscription only.

Markets that are especially eager to receive manuscripts from young people are preceded with an asterisk (*). Markets that require a prepaid fee (except for services accessed by computer) are marked with a dollar sign ($). More information regarding on-line opportunities can be found in the text preceding the on-line markets at the end of this chapter.

Information for each listing was provided directly from the market through our survey and is as current as possible.

The following chart and sample market listing will help explain the information contained within each section.

MARKET LISTING CHART

SECTION	YOU WILL FIND	PAY SPECIAL ATTENTION TO
1	Name of Market. Mailing address for artwork, manuscripts, guidelines, and sample copies. Brief description including how often it is published, the age and interests of its readers.	Who reads this publication and the general theme followed in each issue.
2	Types of art, photographs, and written material that are considered for publication. Specific material that is not accepted.	Any special columns or departments open exclusively to young artists and photographers. Any specific types of material that are never used.
3	More detailed information to help you create acceptable artwork and photographs. Payments offered; rights purchased. Types of media that may be used; specifics of size and style. Availability of guidelines and samples.	Any special instruction for submitting artwork, photographs, and manuscripts. Whether you need to include a signed statement from your parent or teacher or guardian.
4	Advice and helpful tips especially for young artists and photographers, quoted directly from the editor.	What the editors say they do and do not want from young artists and photographers.
5	Subscription rates. Subscription mailing address when it differs from the editorial office.	Included as an extra service for young people, parents, and teachers.

SAMPLE MARKET LISTING

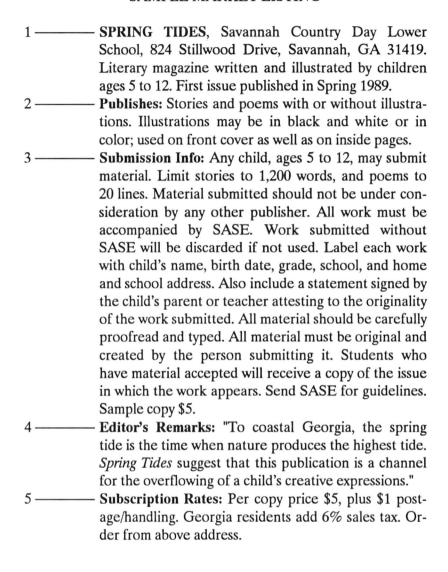

1 —————— **SPRING TIDES**, Savannah Country Day Lower School, 824 Stillwood Drive, Savannah, GA 31419. Literary magazine written and illustrated by children ages 5 to 12. First issue published in Spring 1989.

2 —————— **Publishes:** Stories and poems with or without illustrations. Illustrations may be in black and white or in color; used on front cover as well as on inside pages.

3 —————— **Submission Info:** Any child, ages 5 to 12, may submit material. Limit stories to 1,200 words, and poems to 20 lines. Material submitted should not be under consideration by any other publisher. All work must be accompanied by SASE. Work submitted without SASE will be discarded if not used. Label each work with child's name, birth date, grade, school, and home and school address. Also include a statement signed by the child's parent or teacher attesting to the originality of the work submitted. All material should be carefully proofread and typed. All material must be original and created by the person submitting it. Students who have material accepted will receive a copy of the issue in which the work appears. Send SASE for guidelines. Sample copy $5.

4 —————— **Editor's Remarks:** "To coastal Georgia, the spring tide is the time when nature produces the highest tide. *Spring Tides* suggest that this publication is a channel for the overflowing of a child's creative expressions."

5 —————— **Subscription Rates:** Per copy price $5, plus $1 postage/handling. Georgia residents add 6% sales tax. Order from above address.

CHAPTER SIX
The Market List

* THE ACORN, 1530 7th Street, Rock Island, IL 61201. Publication targeted to young writers in grades K-12, as well as teachers seeking outlets for student writers.

Publishes: Artwork may be submitted with fiction manuscripts, nonfiction articles, and fillers.

Submission Info: Do not submit artwork larger than 4" X 6". Always put name and address on all artwork and manuscripts, as well as your grade. Fiction and nonfiction should be approximately 200 words, no more than 500 words. Poems, any style, may not exceed 30 lines. Manuscripts and artwork without SASE will not be acknowledged or returned. Sample copy $1.

Editor's Remarks: "Always put name and home address of young author, even if manuscripts are submitted by a teacher. Either send a cover letter with this information or be sure it is on the manuscript. School name and address is optional."

Subscription Rates: One year (six issues) $5.

*$ AGORA: THE MAGAZINE FOR GIFTED STUDENTS, AG Publications, P.O. Box 10975, Raleigh, NC 27605. For advanced secondary school students and their teachers with English emphasis but interdisciplinary approach.

Publishes: Short stories, poems, art, photography, and games. Also essays with an interdisciplinary approach.

Submission Info: Writers in grades 7-12 preferred. All submissions printed are copyrighted by magazine but author also retains rights. No payment for submissions at this time. Brochure with details available for SASE.

Editor's Remarks: "Submissions must be from students who subscribe to *Agora* or who attend a school subscribing to a class set."

Subscription Rates: Individual subscription (four issues during school year) $10. Class set (twenty or more to one address) $8. Teacher's supplement $20; free with class set.

BEAR ESSENTIAL NEWS FOR KIDS, 2406 S. 24th Street, Suite E-240, Phoenix, AZ 85034-6822. A monthly publication (of Garrett Communications, Inc.) for children in grade levels K-8. Emphasis is placed on ages 8-12, grades 4-8.

Publishes: Has need for photos, cartoon humor, news features, and interviews on a regular basis. Article reprints are sometimes considered.

Submission Info: SASE must accompany submissions. Material should be typed with sufficient margins and include the writer's name, address, and age. Topics of interest include creative educational pieces; world news as it affects children; unique school projects; profiles of achievements by children; current events in 4th grade terminology; family entertainment features; science, youth sports, and health; hobbies; pet and pet care; cartoon humor; and educational trivia or puzzles.

Editor's Remarks: "Most articles, photos, and illustrations are currently assigned in advance. Feature assignment queries should be requested in writing through Executive Editor Robert Henschen. Our Essential News Network is also looking for stringers in major metropolitan areas."

BITTERROOT POETRY MAGAZINE, P.O. Box 489, Spring Glen, NY 12483-0489. An international poetry magazine appearing three times a year.

Publishes: "Good poetry." Submit three to four poems with #10 SASE. Payment, one copy. Rights revert to author after publication. Send unpublished poems only. Artwork accepted if in black and white or line drawings. Payment, one copy.

Submission Info: Address artwork to Rivke Katz, Art Editor; poems to Menke Katz, Editor.

Editor's Remarks: "It's best to see our magazine to know what we use. Poems are considered better if the how is stressed rather than what is said. Avoid wordiness, cliches, try to be as original as possible. Avoid over-used rhymes, or use no rhyme."

Subscription Rates: One year (three issues) $10. Two years $18. Three years $25. Sample copy is $4.

* **CABOODLE: BY KIDS FOR KIDS**, P.O. Box 1049, Portland, IN 47371. Quarterly publication for children 6 to 12.

Publishes: Readers are invited to write and illustrate their own ideas and send them to the editors. Interested in seeing student-produced stories, articles, poems, and puzzles.

Submission Info: Please send the following information along with any submission: name, complete address, age, current grade, grade when material was written, parent's name, school, school address, teacher's name, and a statement signed by the parent or guardian stating that the material is original and the student's own work. Enclose SASE with sufficient postage if you wish material to be sent back to you. Children receive two free copies of the magazine in which their work is published. Sample copy $2.50.

Editor's Remarks: "We are unable to write to tell contributors whether we have accepted or rejected their work if they do not send SASE."

Subscription Rates: One year (four quarterly issues) $10.

* CHILDREN'S PLAYMATE, 1100 Waterway Blvd., P.O. Box 567, Indianapolis, IN 46206. Monthly publication for children 5 to 7 from the Children's Better Health Institute. Stresses health-related themes or ideas, including nutrition, safety, exercise, or proper health habits.

Publishes: From readers, original poems, original artwork, and jokes and riddles. Does not publish stories written by readers.

Submission Info: Poetry must have been made up by the reader himself. Artwork must be pictures drawn by the reader. Jokes and riddles can be favorite ones readers have heard. (Sorry, no material can be returned.) No payment is made for published reader material. All contributors may purchase copies in which their work appears at a reduced rate. Send SASE for guidelines. Sample copies available for 75¢. Submissions should be limited to young people ages 6-8.

Editor's Remarks: "Unfortunately, because of the many thousands of contributions we receive, we are not able to publish everything sent in to us."

Subscription Rates: One year $11.95. Special rate of $9.97 is usually offered in every issue.

COBBLESTONE, 30 Grove Street, Peterborough, NH 03458. Monthly history magazine for young people. Monthly themes followed.

Publishes: Artwork related to monthly theme in the form of drawings, puzzles, mazes, craft projects, etc. Only accepts feature-length material if it relates to an upcoming theme. Uses authentic historical and biographical fiction, adventure, retold legends, etc., relating to theme. Supplemental nonfiction that includes subjects directly and indirectly related to theme. Activities including crafts, recipes, woodworking projects, and others that can be done either alone or with adult supervision. Poetry, puzzles and games. No wordfinds. Uses crosswords and other word puzzles with the vocabulary of the issue's theme. Also mazes and picture puzzles.

Submission Info: All submissions *must* relate to a monthly theme. Theme lists and writer's guidelines available for SASE. Refer to specific guidelines for advice on submitting a query. Pay varies depending on type of material accepted. Sample copy $3.95 plus 7½" X 10½" (or larger) self-addressed envelope with $1.05 postage.

Editor's Remarks: "Unfortunately, we do not have enough space to regularly publish students' work other than the letters, drawings, and short poems sent to *Cobblestone* for 'Dear Ebenezer.' We occasionally have contests that involve creative writing. Keep an eye out for these contests. All submissions for feature material, from students and adults alike, is evaluated equally.

Subscription Rates: One year $22.95. Also on some newsstands.

* **CREATIVE KIDS**, GCT Inc., P.O. Box 6448, Mobile, AL 36660. A full-size magazine by kids, for kids.

Publishes: Stories, prose, poetry, plays, artwork, photography, games, and music from young people ages 5 to 18. Work must be original and submitted only to *Creative Kids* (no simultaneous submissions). Material must be nonracist, nonsexist, and nonviolent.

Submission Info: Cover letter is necessary and should include name, address, birthdate, school, school address, and signature by parent or teacher authenticating originality, along with a photo (if available). Send SASE for detailed guidelines. Sample copy $3.

Editor's Remarks: "*Creative Kids* is the only award-winning, full size magazine with all of its contents contributed by gifted, creative, and talented youngsters. It includes children's work that represents their ideas, questions, fears, concerns, and pleasures. The prime purpose is to encourage children to strive for a product that is good enough for publication. It requires effort, discipline, and a sense of responsibility. The reward is to know that the material has appeared in print and is shared with thousands of readers."

Subscription Rates: One year $24. New reader rate for one year $17.97. Schools and libraries may request a free sample copy by sending a request on school or library stationery.

DIALOGUE, 3100 Oak Park Avenue, Berwyn, IL 60402. Quarterly magazine for the visually impaired, published in braille, large print, cassette, and on recorded discs playable on Talking Book machines for an audience of blind and visually impaired adults.

Publishes: Fiction and nonfiction general interest material. Photos and artwork.

Submission Info: *Dialogue* cannot consider the work of writers who are not visually impaired. Because it is a service organization, new writers are asked to include a brief statement regarding their visual impairment with their first submission. Send for guidelines regarding photos and artwork. Free-lance writer's guidelines are available in regular print, in large print, in braille, and on cassette. Persons wishing them on cassette should send a C-90. Sample copies are free. Be sure to request which edition you prefer. Send SASE for regular print guidelines.

Editor's Remarks: "We write for a general interest adult audience and rarely use fiction or articles written from a juvenile point of view. A young person should study the kind of material we publish in *Dialogue* and might break into our market best with poetry or a contribution for one of our regular departments such as 'ABAPITA' or 'Vox Pop.'"

Subscription Rates: All editions − braille, large print, cassette, or recorded discs for one year $20. Back copies are donated to agencies, schools, and blind individuals throughout the world."

FACES, 30 Grove Street, Peterborough, NH 03458. Monthly history magazine about people.

Publishes: Variety of feature articles and in-depth and personal accounts relating to monthly themes. Word length: 800-1,200. Also supplemental nonfiction, 200-800 words. Includes subjects directly and indirectly related to themes. Also some fiction, activities, photos, poetry, puzzles, and games − all with a connection to an upcoming theme.

Submission Info: Operates on a by-assignment basis, but welcomes ideas and suggestions in outline form. Ideas should be submitted at least six months prior to the publication date. Pays on individual basis. Guidelines with theme list available for SASE. Sample copy $3.75 plus 7½" X 10½" (or larger) self-addressed envelope with 85¢ postage.

Editor's Remarks: "Unfortunately, we do not have enough space to regularly publish students' work other than the letters, drawings, and short poems sent to *Faces* for 'Letters Page.' We occasionally have contests which involve creative writing. Keep an eye out for these contests. All submissions for feature material, from students and adults alike, is evaluated equally.

Subscription Rates: Available by subscription. Write to above address for rates.

* FLYING PENCIL PRESS, P.O. Box 7667, Elgin, IL 60121. Independent publishing house dedicated to the writing and artwork of children ages 8 to 14. New theme explored each year.

Publishes: Annual anthology of children's work (fiction, nonfiction, poems, art and cartoons) in quality paperback books for the general bookstore market. Art must be black and white line drawings on 8" X 10" or smaller paper. Includes cartoons (1 to 8 frames), or drawings related to theme.

Submission Info: Prefers typewritten manuscripts but will accept handwritten material if it is clear and readable. Artwork, illustrations, and cartoons should be on unlined white paper. Manuscripts must be aimed toward an upcoming theme. Material *must* be the original work of the submitting author or artist. Does not accept tracings or freehand copying of already published artwork. Writings copied from published books or magazines will not be considered. Enclose SASE if you wish material returned if not accepted. Be sure to keep a copy of your material in case original is lost in handling or mailing. Replies by mail in four to six weeks if your work is accepted. Payment may be offered. Guidelines and theme sheet available for SASE. Artists who would like to illustrate work done by other students should send several relevant samples of their artwork plus a cover letter stating their desire to draw illustrations for The Flying Pencil Press. Be sure to include an appropriate size envelope and adequate postage if you wish your artwork returned. Artists, *do not fold* artwork; send it flat and protect it with a sturdy piece of cardboard. Upcoming themes include: Fantasy, magic, mystical, or strange things; holidays.

Editor's Remarks: "We are looking for original, honest, imaginative, bright work. Be yourself and write, draw, create from your own ideas and feelings. Be sure to send material appropriate for a current theme. We hope to hear from you soon."

Subscription Rates: Write for information, all proceeds go to publish future editions.

* FUTURIFIC MAGAZINE, 280 Madison Avenue, New York, NY 10016. Published twelve times a year by Futurific, Inc., a nonprofit educational organization dedicated to finding a better understanding of the future. Not related to any other organization, corporate, government, religious or otherwise.

Publishes: Material that is an analysis of any issue in current events. All material must show what *improvements* are coming in the near future. No gloom and doom stories, and do not try to tell readers how they should live their lives. Wants material that tells what *will* happen. Artwork must be relevant to magazine's overall theme.

Submission Info: Buys one-time rights. Payment is negotiated. Material will only be returned with SASE. Presently only black and white photos and artwork are used. Sample copies available for $5, which includes processing, postage, and handling.

Editor's Remarks: "Readership consists of anyone interested in the future and who is uncomfortable at the lack of research dealing with it and the lack of accurate foresight available. We are only interested in how correct you are in reporting on the future. Fantasy must be wed to reality. Remember, we are not as interested in your age as your correct view of where the world is heading."

Subscription Rates: One year for individuals $40; institutions $80.

* **HIGHLIGHTS FOR CHILDREN**, 803 Church Street, Honesdale, PA 18431. Published monthly for youngsters ages 2 to 12.

Publishes: Accepts poems, drawings, and stories from readers. Also runs two unfinished stories a year to which readers submit their creative endings. For writers 16 or older, also reviews submissions of short stories, factual features, puzzles, party plans, crafts, finger plays, and action plays. Seldom buys verse.

Submission Info: For writers up to age 15, make drawings in black and white. For a special feature, "Creatures Nobody Has Ever Seen," drawings are sent in color. Prose usually runs no more than 250 words. Acknowledges all material submitted. However, material is not returned, so *do not enclose SASE*. No payment is made for contributions from writers 15 or under. For writers over 16, consult regular free-lance guidelines available free. Fiction should not be more than 900 words; pays 8¢ and up per word. Science and factual articles within 900 words bring $75 and up. Other material brings $25 and up. Those 16 and over should send complete manuscript with SASE for its possible return. All submissions need to include name, age, and complete home address. Personal photo is unnecessary.

Subscription Rates: One year $19.95. Three years $49.95. Write: *Highlights for Children*, 2300 West Fifth Avenue, P.O. Box 269, Columbus, OH 43216.

* **HUMPTY DUMPTY'S MAGAZINE**, 1100 Waterway Blvd., P.O. Box 567, Indianapolis, IN 46206. Monthly publication for children ages 4 to 6 from the Children's Better Health Institute. Stresses health-related themes or ideas including nutrition, safety, exercise, or proper health habits.

Publishes: From readers: artwork or pictures drawn or colored by the readers themselves.

Submission Info: Send drawn or colored pictures or other artwork. Include SASE if you wish material not accepted to be returned. NO payment is made for published reader material. All contributors may purchase copies in which their work appears at a reduced rate. Sample copies available for 75¢. Submission should be limited to children ages 4-6.

Editor's Remarks: "Unfortunately, because of the many thousands of contributions we receive, we are not able to publish everything sent in to us. We do hope that parents and teachers explain to the children that failure to get their pictures published does not mean that the artwork wasn't well done. It simply means that we didn't have room."

Subscription Rates: One year $11.95. Special rate of $9.97 is usually offered in every issue.

* **INSECT WORLD**, Young Entomologist's Society, Inc., 1915 Peggy Place, Lansing, MI 48910-2553. Gary A. Dunn, editor. Bimonthly, newsletter for youth (and their teachers) interested in insects and spiders.

Publishes: Original photographs (black and white only), line drawings, cartoons, and illustrations of insects and spiders. Also original informative articles, essays, stories, poems, jokes, puzzles, games, and activity ideas on insects and spiders.

Submission Info: Manuscripts should be typed *single-spaced*. Photos must be in black and white. All drawings, maps, charts, etc. should be done in black ink and proportioned to fit journal's 5½" X 8½" size. Allow half-inch margin all around. Whenever possible, state both common and scientific names for species mentioned in articles. Also, for the benefit of those living in other countries, identify state/province and country when giving locality information. Guidelines available in each issue or for SASE. Sample copy $1. No compensation given. Articles by members will be given priority, otherwise manuscripts are used on a first-come, first-serve basis. Receipt of all materials is acknowledged in writing.

Editor's Remarks: "*Insect World* is specially designed for kids and adults (parents, teachers, naturalists, and 'bug club' leaders) who have an interest in insects. While it is produced with 6-14 year old youth in mind, it has been used successfully by parents with 3-5 year olds and by teachers and youth group leaders."

Subscription Rates: Nonmembers one year $18. Members $6.

* **IN TOUCH,** P.O. Box 50434, Indianapolis, IN 46250. Weekly magazine published by Wesley Press in conjunction with the Wesley Biblical Series Curriculum to reinforce each week's session.

Publishes: Nonfiction including Christian testimonies, observations on contemporary issues, how-to articles, humor, interviews with famous or newsworthy Christians. Fiction needs include a true experience told in fiction style, humorous fiction, or a C.S. Lewis-type allegory. Uses *very little* poetry, cartoons, or puzzles. Include photos if available. Needs *Seventeen*- and *Campus Life*-type cover shots and close-ups of faces.

Submission Info: Photos should be black and white glossies, 8" X 10". Length for both fiction and nonfiction is 500-1,200 words. Send seasonal material at least nine months in advance. Manuscripts need to be typed. Follow standard formats. Be sure to include word count. Indicate what rights are being offered: one-time, simultaneous, or reprint. Usually buys one-time rights. Pays 4¢ a word for first rights; 2¢ a word for reprints. Photos are purchased separately and pay from $20-$40. Sample copy and detailed guidelines available for SASE.

Editor's Remarks: "Understand the official *In Touch* password: 'Wesleyan-Arminian-evangelical-holiness manuscript'. Roughly translated that means articles should reflect a joy and excitement in a personal relationship with God. We attempt to encourage a biblical lifestyle, witnessing, sexual purity, and abstinence from all things harmful to the body and soul, with being 'preachy.'"

Subscription Rates: One year $9.25 (subject to change).

* INTERNATIONAL READERS' NEWSLETTER, c/o Marsha James, Newsletter Coordinator, The Perfection Form Company, 10520 New York Avenue, Des Moines, IA, USA 50322. Newspaper format publication published four times during the school year featuring a wide variety of writing and art by and for secondary school students. Also encourages applications for student editor positions.

Publishes: Visual interpretations of fiction or nonfiction (cartoons, scenes, collages, etc.), provided they meet specific publication guidelines. Also publishes a variety of written material in which students express their feelings about something they have read. Submissions may be *about* fiction (novels, short stories, plays), nonfiction (speeches, essays, biographies, articles), or poetry. May also be about a movie that is based on a specific book. Responses can take one of many forms, such as a "literary letter" to the author, a friend, the editors, your teacher, your family, etc. Or you can write a letter directly to a character. Feelings can also be shared in the form of poetry or art. Or compose a dialogue between characters.

Submission Info: Artwork must be clearly connected to a specific fiction or nonfiction piece the student has read. Must be done on white paper with black ink or charcoal. Submit original artwork, no copies. (Note: artwork is not returned.) Do not bend or fold artwork. Use standard format when mailing. Photos must elaborate or depict fiction or nonfiction. Send black and white photos only. If possible, include a recent photo of yourself. Artists are limited to four submissions per year. All submissions of writing and/or art and photos *must* be accompanied by a "Permission to Publish" form available in each issue. Complete guidelines also available in each issue.

Will consider any type of response *as long as it is connected to fiction or nonfiction* that has been read by the young person submitting. Include the title and author of the reading or film you are responding to.

Editor's Remarks: "The most important criterion is that the submission *must* be a response to a work of fiction or nonfiction that the student has read or viewed. Editorial changes may be made to smooth grammar, spelling, or punctuation. Some writings may be shortened. But your message will not be changed."

Subscription Rates: One year for one to ten subscriptions $11.95 each. Save 50% on orders of more than ten subscriptions. May also subscribe for half year (two issues, March & May) for $5.95. In U.S. call (800) 831-4190 for more information. Outside U.S. call (712) 644-2831.

* IOWA WOMAN, P.O. Box 680, Iowa City, IA 52244. Quarterly magazine published since 1979 by Iowa Woman Endeavors, Inc., a nonprofit, independent educational service organization run by volunteers with a primarily midwestern readership.

Publishes: Cover art by Iowa women only. Small line drawings, cartoons, and black and white photographs considered by all women for use inside the magazine. Photographic "portfolios" and various writtten material such as short stories, essays, book reviews, poetry, etc. are also considered. Has a special column for young women and girls called "Under 21."

Submission Info: Cartoons and small drawings should be submitted in camera-ready format. Send SASE to receive detailed guidelines for artwork and manuscripts. Sample copy $5. Artists with art inside the magazine receive two complimentary copies. Cover art artists recive two copies plus one year subscription.

Editor's Remarks: "We have a constant need for small line drawings and cartoons to enrich the pages of text, and will also consider black and white photographic portfolios."

Subscription Rates: One year (four issues) $15.

* KIDSART, P.O. Box 274, Mt. Shasta, CA 96067. Publication and program with international participation, which presents ideas and encourages children to participate in a variety of writing and artwork projects with reproducible worksheets in art history and art appreciation.

Publishes: Articles from children or adults about any "hands-on" art projects suitable for elementary school children. Samples of finished project and/or photos appreciated. Also publishes child-made artwork (drawings, printmaking, painting, etc.).

Submission Info: Originals will be returned if SASE with sufficient postage is included with submission. Photos of child-made artwork are also okay, as are photocopies of pen or pencil drawings. Include full name of child artist/writer so credit can be given. Send SASE to receive more information.

Editor's Remarks: "Note about payment: We do not pay for articles or illustrations (yet), but we do extend free subscriptions to everyone whose art is published, and to all writers whose articles are used, or whose submission inspires an activity published."

Subscription Rates: One year (four issues) $8.

* **KOALA CLUB NEWS**, Zoological Society of San Diego, Inc., P.O. Box 551, San Diego, CA 92112. Quarterly publication for children age 15 and under.

Publishes: Accepts original drawings, black and white photos, poems, riddles, and stories for "Porky Pine's Pen Pals" section. The material must be about animals.

Submission Info: Use standard format. No submissions returned. No payment is made for accepted submissions, but will send a free *Zoo Babies* book to young writers whose submissions are published. Include name, age, and address with each submission. Write with SASE for information about obtaining a sample copy.

Subscription Rates: *Koala Club News* is available to members of the Society's Koala Club. Membership dues of $9 per year include unlimited entrance to the San Diego Zoo, the San Diego Wild Animal Park, and the quarterly publication.

LANDMARK EDITIONS, INC., P.O. Box 4469, Kansas City, MO 64127. Publishes original books geared to students.

Publishes: Most books published have been submitted through their sponsored contest. *Occasionally*, will accept a book manuscript geared to student readers.

Submission Info: See contest listing. For submissions other than for contest, it's best to send a query letter with SASE.

Editor's Remarks: "We primarily seek manuscripts through our annual *National Written & Illustrated By . . . Awards Contest*."

Subscription Rates: Published books sold through distributors, bookstores, and direct mail. To order direct call (816) 241-4919.

* LISTEN, CELEBRATING POSITIVE CHOICES, 12501 Old Columbia Pike, Silver Spring, MD 20904. A monthly publication for teens and young adults encouraging the development of good habits and high ideals of physical and mental health.

Publishes: Special column for teens called "Graffiti," which uses short, well-written, thought-provoking poems, stories, and essays from teen writers. Also uses factual features or opinion essays with or without accompanying quality photos; narratives based on true-life incidents, poetry, puzzles, and cartoons.

Submission Info: Submissions for "Graffiti" should include age, grade, school, etc; no personal photos. Poetry should not be longer than 20 lines; stories and essays 300-500 words. Address to "Graffiti" in care of *Listen* magazine. Include SASE. Send for free writer's guidelines and tip sheet. Samples available for $1 and large manila envelope with SASE. Pays $10 for poems; $15-$20 for stories and essays. Varying rates for other material.

Editor's Remarks: "*Listen* is circulated in public high schools and junior high schools, so religious material is not suitable."

Subscription Rates: One year (twelve monthly issues) $16.95. Higher outside U.S. Send check or money order to *Listen*, P.O. Box 7000, Boise, ID 83707. Also available in many school libraries.

* THE MCGUFFEY WRITER, 5128 Westgate Drive, Oxford, OH 45056. Magazine of children's own writing published three times a year for nationwide audience.

Publishes: Short stories, essays, poems, and songs. Also cartoons and illustrations done in black and white. Each issue follows a pre-determined theme. Open to students K-12.

Submission Info: Manuscripts submitted will be acknowledged but are not returned. Please enclose SASE. Students must list name, grade level, school, and address on *every* submitted page. Do not include photo. A teacher, supervisor, or responsible adult must sign the initial page for verification. Typed or handwritten submissions are equally welcome as long as they are readable; however, the child's original copy is preferred. Due to limited space, excerpts may be taken from work that is longer than 2 double-spaced typewritten pages. Guidelines available at the above address. Sample copy $3. Guidelines, helpful hints, and deadlines are given in each issue.

Editor's Remarks: "Items are accepted on the basis of merit, originality, and appropriateness to the overall balance and theme of the issue."

Subscription Rates: One year single subscription (three issues — Fall, Winter, Spring) $7.50. Institutional rates (for three complete yearly subscriptions sent to a single address) $15. One year patron subscription (helps to defray costs) send $25. Patrons are listed on the inside of the spring issue.

* MERLYN'S PEN: THE NATIONAL MAGAZINE OF STUDENT WRITING, Grades 7-10, P.O. Box 1058, East Greenwich, RI 02818. Toll free: (800) 247-2027. In Rhode Island (401) 885-5175. Magazine written entirely by students in grades 7-10. Four issues published during school year.

Publishes: Stories, plays, poems, essays on important issues, review letters, word games, opinions, critiques of writing in magazine. Black and white or color art and photos welcome by students grades 7-10. Also considers puzzles. Letters to the editor are welcome.

Submission Info: A statement of originality must be signed for each accepted piece. Published authors and artists receive three complimentary issues that contain their work and a small gift. Guidelines for submitting literature and art must be followed exactly. Each submission receives a response within twelve weeks. All submissions (art and literature) *must* include a large, self-addressed stamped envelope and a cover sheet with author's name, grade, age, home address, home phone number, school name, school address, school phone, and supervising teacher's name. Manuscripts must be typed, double-spaced with extra-wide margins. Manuscripts should be stapled and the author's name should be on every page. Artwork should be in black ink or charcoal on white paper (no lead pencil or blue ink). Color work (oils, pastels, watercolor, etc.) can only be considered for the cover. Photographs are welcome. Art work should not be folded or matted, but cardboard backing should be used in the envelope. Include all necessary information (see above) and SASE with adequate postage. No personal photos necessary.

Editor's Remarks: "*Merlyn's Pen* considers all kinds of literature written by students in grades 7-10. The magazine seeks manuscripts that grip the readers' interest and stir the heart and mind. The best advice we can offer is: Write what you know and revise, revise, revise! Make every word count."

Subscription Rates: Rates for one year (four issues during school year) $14.95 each for one to ten subscriptions; $7.95 each (eleven to twenty subs); $5.95 each (twenty-one or more subs).

* NATIONAL GEOGRAPHIC WORLD, National Geographic Society, 1145 17th NW, Washington, DC 20036. A monthly picture magazine for readers age 8 and older.

Publishes: Children's art.

Submission Info: *World* is a highly specialized market for regular photos and text. Read several back issues to see the type of children's art work accepted. Send SASE for specific guidelines before submitting material. All contributors receive three complimentary copies of the issue in which their work appears. Additional copies may be purchased at a reduced rate.

Editor's Remarks: "*World* editors will *not* review poetry or fiction manuscripts. Address story proposals to Submissions Editor."

Subscription Rates: Available through National Geographic Society.

* **NEWSCURRENTS,** Knowledge Unlimited, Inc., P.O. Box 52, Madison, WI 53701. (800) 356-2303. A weekly current events discussion program for students in grades 3 to 12.

Publishes: Editorial cartoons on any subject of national or international interest created by students in grades 3 to 12. Selected cartoons appear in *NewsCurrents*.

Submission Info: Use black ink on white paper, and draw and letter in bold lines. If possible, draw cartoon in a slightly horizontal format. Don't "clutter" cartoon with too many different ideas. Detailed guidelines available. *NewsCurrents* editors *do not* send materials back.

Editor's Remarks: "Editorial cartoons submitted are automatically entered in annual "Student Editorial Cartoon Contest."

Subscription Rates: Write or call for rates.

* **OUR FAMILY,** Box 249, Battleford, Saskatchewan, Canada S0M 0E0. Monthly magazine published for a national readership of Catholic families, most of whom have children in grade school, high school, or college.

Publishes: Nonfiction related to the following areas: people at home; people in relation to God; people at recreation; people at work; people in the world; biography (profiles about Christians whose living of Christian values has had a positive effect on their contemporaries); and inspirational articles. Also spiritual reflection; humorous anecdotes; poetry on human/spiritual themes; cartoons (family-type); photos. *No fiction.*

Submission Info: Send for theme list and detailed guidelines for nonfiction and photos by enclosed SAE and 45¢ Canadian postage or IRC (International Reply Coupon). (Average cost to return manuscript is 99¢ in Canadian funds.) Sample copy is $2.50.

Editor's Remarks: "The majority of our readers are adults. If young people write for us, they must understand that they are writing and competing in an adult market. Since our publication stresses the personal experience approach, young people could find a slot in our publication by writing as teenagers focusing on teenage concerns. We make no distinction of age. If a particular article/poem/filler effectively reaches a certain segment of the family, we are pleased to purchase it for publication in our magazine."

Subscription Rates: Write for information.

POETIC PAGE, P.O. Box 71192, Madison Heights, MI 48071. Bi-monthly poetry publication with primarily adult readership; has children's poetry page.

Publishes: Artwork accepted, but seeks high quality. Poetry is limited to 24 lines.

Submission Info: Black and white line drawings preferred. Send cover letter with submission, be sure to include the age of the poet or artist. No photo necessary. Work *must* be author's own. All rights remain with poet after publication. Send *all* material to: Denise Martinson, Editor. All submissions *must* include SASE. Sample copy $1.50.

Editor's Remarks: "We are a small press publication with a readership of poets, editors, and ten libraries. We use one or two poems by young writers per issue and want work to be appropriate for this age group − 6 to 15."

Subscription Rates: One year (six issues) $7.50.

* SHOE TREE: THE LITERARY MAGAZINE BY AND FOR YOUNG WRITERS, 215 Valle del Sol Drive, Santa Fe, NM 87501. Published by the National Association for Young Writers. Both writers and readers are from 6 to 15 years old.

Publishes: In search of well-written stories; nonfiction essays, particularly personal narratives; and good poetry, but not haiku or cinquain. Photos and artwork are welcome. Note: *Shoe Tree* often decides on artists by viewing samples of their work. If you would like to be considered as an illustrator for *Shoe Tree*, submit several samples of your best work, along with your request, to editor Sheila Cowing.

Submission Info: Submissions must be accompanied by the writer's name, age, school and teacher's name, and a statement of authenticity signed by the writer and a parent, guardian, or teacher. Submission guidelines available for SASE. Sample copy is $5, but is free to educators and librarians.

Editor's Remarks: "We are looking for good writing straight from the heart. Fantasy and science fiction must be grounded in reality. Poems must touch. Often the best method to achieve these goals is to write from personal experience."

Subscription Rates: One year (three issues) $15. Two years $28. Three years $42. Classroom discounts available. Subscription services: NAYW Membership Services, P.O. Box 3001, Dept. YW, Denville, NJ 07834.

SHOFAR, Senior Publications Ltd., 43 Northcote Drive, Melville, NY 11747. Published October through May for Jewish children ages 8 to 13. Managing Editor: Gerald H. Grayson.

Publishes: Nonfiction, fiction (500-700 words), poetry, photos, puzzles, games, cartoons. (Artwork on assignment only.) *All material must be on a Jewish theme.* Special holiday issues. Black and white, color prints purchased with manuscripts at additional fee.

Submission Info: Complete manuscripts preferred. Queries welcome. Submit holiday theme pieces at least four months in advance. Will consider photocopied and simultaneous submissions. Buys first North American serial rights or first serial rights. Pays on publication: 7¢ per word plus five copies. Reports in six to eight weeks. Send a 9" X 12" SASE with 90¢ postage for free sample copy.

Editor's Remarks: "All material must be on a Jewish theme."

* **SKIPPING STONES**, c/o Aprovecho Institute, 80574 Hazelton Road, Cottage Grove, OR 97424. International, nonprofit quarterly children's magazine featuring writing and art by children 5 to 13. Writing may be submitted in *any* language and from any country.

Publishes: Original artwork, photos, poems, stories, magic tricks, recipes, science experiments, songs, games, movie and book reviews, writings about your background, culture, religion, interests and experiences, etc. May also send questions for other readers to answer or ask your pen pal to send a letter. Submissions are welcome in *all* languages. (Work is published in the language submitted.)

Submission Info: Prefers original work (keep your own copy). Short pieces preferred. Also prefers that pieces include your age and a description of your background. Can be typed or handwritten or handprinted. Artwork in black and white, pen and ink are preferred. Those who have material published receive a copy of the issue in which their work appears. Material in *Skipping Stones* is not copyrighted for exclusive use. Reproduction for educational use is encouraged. Guidelines available, please enclose SASE or SAE with IRC if possible. Guidelines also published in each issue. Sample copy $3.75. (Also enclose SASE with submissions if at all possible.) Address submissions to either Arun Toke or Amy Klauke, editors.

Editor's Remarks: "*Skipping Stones* is primarily a place for young people of diverse backgrounds to share their particular experiences and expressions. Our goal is to reach children around the world, in economically disadvantaged as well as in privileged families, including underrepresented and special populations within North America. We invite you to suggest ways your organization might network with *Skipping Stones*, perhaps through sharing insights on possible submission of material, outreach, or ideas on the contents or format. In turn, if your group supports projects relevant to children, send this information to us and we will do our best to let our readers know about your work.

Subscription Rates: In U.S. one year $15; two years $28. Foreign (Canadian & overseas) one year $20 in U.S. funds. Third World libraries & schools, or low income families in U.S., may purchase one year subscription for $10. Free subscriptions available when situation warrants. Contact editorial office for information.

*$ SMALL FRY ORIGINALS, 2700 S. Westmoreland Avenue, P.O. Box 769045, Dallas, TX 75376-9045. [Author's note: Not a true market, but a unique method of displaying children's art.]

Publishes: Children's artwork in preserved form on melamine plates, thermoplastic insulated mugs, and photo plates.

Submission Info: Send $3.95 for "Small Fry Plates" or "Color Photo Plates" kit; $2.95 for "Small Fry Mugs." Each kit will do fifty designs and includes fifty sheets of paper, twelve markers, instructions, order forms (for finished product) and shipping labels. It takes approximately four to six weeks from the time prepared artwork is submitted until finished items are shipped. For Mother's Day and Christmas, expect six weeks.

Editor's Remarks: "Please use only our markers, or we can't guarantee the results!"

* SNAKE RIVER REFLECTIONS, 1863 Bitterroot Drive, Twin Falls, ID 83301-3561. Formerly called *Writing Pursuits,* Bill White, Editor. Published monthly except July and August. Target audience includes writers of all ages.

Publishes: Short articles on tips for writers, poetry, notices of contests and publications, cartoons on writing topics, news of writing events, credits of subscribers, and news of writing chapters.

Submission Info: Short articles of one page or less are preferred. Poems should be limited to 30 lines. A cover letter optional. Include SASE with adequate postage with all inquiries and submissions. Rights revert back to author after publication. Payment at this time is in copies only. Response time is two weeks. Material will be returned only if SASE is included. *No* simultaneous submissions accepted. Sample copy available for SASE with 25¢ postage.

Editor's Remarks: "Cartoons and fillers on writing topics are especially needed."

Subscription Rates: One year (ten issues) $5.

* **SPRING TIDES**, Savannah Country Day Lower School, 824 Stillwood Drive, Savannah, GA 31419. Literary magazine written and illustrated by children ages 5 to 12. First issue published in Spring 1989.

Publishes: Stories and poems with or without illustrations. Illustrations may be black and white or in color, used on front cover as well as on inside pages.

Submission Info: Any child, ages 5 to 12, may submit material. Limit stories to 1,200 words, and poems to 20 lines. Material submitted should not be under consideration by any other publisher. All work must be accompanied by SASE. Work submitted without SASE will be discarded if not used. Label each work with child's name, birth date, grade, school, and home and school address. Also include a statement signed by the child's parent or teacher attesting to the originality of the work submitted. All material should be carefully proofread and typed. All material must be original and created by the person submitting it. Students who have material accepted will receive a copy of the issue in which the work appears. Send SASE for guidelines. Sample copy $5.

Editor's Remarks: "To Coastal Georgia, the spring tide is the time when nature produces the highest tide. *Spring Tides* suggests that this publication is a channel for the overflowing of a child's creative expressions."

Subscription Rates: Per copy price $5, plus $1 postage/handling. Georgia residents add 6% sales tax. Order from above address.

* **STRAIGHT,** 8121 Hamilton Avenue, Cincinnati, OH 45231. Published quarterly for Christian teens, ages 13-19. Distributed through churches, youth organizations, and private subscriptions.

Publishes: Poetry, stories, and articles from teens. Material must be religious/inspirational in nature and appeal to other teens. Art and photos accepted occasionally.

Submission Info: Submit manuscript on speculation, enclose SASE, birthday (day and year), and Social Security number. Reports in four to six weeks. Buys first and one-time rights; pays 2¢ per word. Samples automatically sent to contributors. Guidelines and sample issues available for SASE. Pays a flat fee for poetry.

Editor's Remarks: "Before you submit, please get to know us. Most teen work that I reject does not fit our editorial slant (religious/inspirational). A look at our guidelines or a sample copy will help teen writers in deciding what to submit. Also, I'd like to encourage teens to write about things they know, but not necessarily 'common' or general topics. We see scores of poems about rainbows and loneliness and friends, but hardly any about 'How I feel about working at McDonalds,' "What happened when I tried something new ...', or "Why I believe in ...' Also, a tacked-on moral does not make a religious story. Make your characters Christian, and the religious slant will take care of itself."

* **THUMBPRINTS,** 928 Gibbs, Caro, MI 48723. Monthly newsletter published by the Thumb Area Writer's Club.

Publishes: Various types of material including poetry, short fiction, articles, essays, information, how-to, opinions, etc. Accepts general topic information but prefers manuscripts that relate to writing, publishing, or the writer's way of life. Also interested in short profiles. Will consider line drawings done in black ink. No photos.

Submission Info: Material must be typed following standard formats. Will consider handwritten material only from writers 12 and under. Send SASE for possible return of manuscript. Stories and articles should be limited to 1,000 words. Prefers items of 500 words or less. Poems should not be longer than 32 lines. Pays in contributor's copies. Sample issue 50¢ each. You do not need to live in Michigan to submit material; however, the work of club members and subscribers will be given first consideration. Send SASE for yearly theme list for ideas.

Editor's Remarks: "We are always looking for manuscripts that inform or warm the hearts of amateur and professional writers alike. You do not need to be a member to submit material."

Subscription Rates: One year for nonmember $8.50.

* TURTLE MAGAZINE FOR PRESCHOOL KIDS, 1100 Waterway Blvd., P.O. Box 567, Indianapolis, IN 46206. Publication for children ages 2 to 5 from the Children's Better Health Institute. Stresses health-related themes or ideas including nutrition, safety, exercise, or proper health habits.

Publishes: From readers: artwork or pictures drawn or colored by the readers themselves.

Submission Info: No payment is made for published reader material. All contributors may purchase copies in which their work appears at a reduced rate. Sample copies available for 75¢. Submissions should be limited to children ages 2-5.

Editor's Remarks: "Unfortunately, because of the many thousands of contributions we receive, we are not able to publish everything sent in to us."

Subscription Rates: One year $11.95. Special rate of $10.95 is usually offered in every issue.

* WEE WISDOM, Unity Village, MO 64065. Christian magazine published ten times yearly for children through 12 years of age.

Publishes: "Writer's Guild" section features poetry and drawings written by children. (Note: the remainder of magazine is published from free-lance fiction written by adults for children.)

Submission Info: Rules for children's submissions to the "Writer's Guild" are given in the beginning section of that column in each issue. (Writer's guidelines are available to adults for SASE.) Poetry and drawing are not returned. An acknowledgment card is sent upon receipt of written work, before any selection is made for publication. If published, a child will receive a certificate of award and a membership card to the Writer's Guild.

Editor's Remarks: "We do not want to see stories from juvenile writers — poetry only. Occasionally we will publish a prose work, but it must be no more than 100 words."

Subscription Rates: Ten issues in U.S. $8; outside U.S. $12.

* WOMBAT: A JOURNAL OF YOUNG PEOPLE'S WRITING AND ART, 365 Ashton Drive, Athens, GA 30606. Publication is comprised of creative work by young people ages 6 to 16. (AUTHOR'S NOTE: At press time *Wombat* had suspended publication but hoped to resume publishing in 1991.)

Publishes: Poetry, short stories, artwork of all kinds, nonfiction articles, cartoons, etc., from young people ages 6 to 16.

Submission Info: Material should include name, age, school, and home address of young person. Photo and brief autobiography for potential use on the "Contributors'" page may be included but is optional. Artwork, illustrations, and picture stories must be originals or exceptionally clear copies of originals. Artwork will be returned only if accompanied by appropriately-sized SASE. Retain copies of written works or send legible, clear copies. Send SASE for guidelines.

Editor's Remarks: "Due to financial problems, we have been forced to temporarily suspend publication of Wombat. However, encouraging creative young people and providing them a market for their work is important to us. We hope to resume publication in 1991. *Please do not send us any manuscripts or artwork before then.* We advise that you send a note asking about our status after January 1, 1991, if you are still interested in our publication. Please enclose SASE for a prompt reply."

Subscription Rates: To be announced after publication is resumed.

*$ WORLD PEN PALS, 1690 Como Avenue, St. Paul, MN 55108. Letter-writing program of the International Institute of Minnesota, a United Way affiliated agency, providing service for all nationalities.

Publishes: Helps link young people ages 12-20 with pen pals around the world. Suggests including the following in pen pal letters: share personal life such as information about your family or school; describe hobbies, holidays, and books; share recipes and art; ask your pen pals questions about their customs, country, schools; take an interest in learning new words and phrases in your pen pal's native language, then use them as you write.

Submission Info: Send name, age, sex, and complete address along with a SASE, plus a $3 service fee. (Fee is $2.50 per request for groups of six or more.) In return, you will receive a foreign pen pal's name and address, plus a suggestions sheet and a newsletter. Do not specify a particular country unless the group is from a language class. Applicants also welcome from Canada. Write to above address with SAE and IRC to receive specific details.

Editor's Remarks: "Each year World Pen Pals links more than 20,000 students, ages 12-20, from 175 countries and territories all over the world, with students in the United States. It does not link students within the U.S. It is fun for students to receive letters from another country. As pen pals correspond, they become good friends even though separated geographically and culturally."

Subscription Rates: Send business-size SASE for application and more information.

WRITER'S GAZETTE, Trouvere Company, Rt.2, Box 290, Eclectic, AL 36024. Quarterly publication about, for, and by writers.

Publishes: Articles about writing. Maximum length 1,500 words. Short stories, any subject. Maximum length 1,500 words. Poetry in any subject, style, or length. Puzzles and quizzes related to writing in any style, and illustrations and cartoons related to writing. Payment varies. Also interested in book reports about new and old books (will list self-published and trade published books). Buys one-time rights. Will consider previously published work.

Submission Info: Use standard formats. Send SASE for guidelines.

Subscription Rates: One year (monthly) $9. Contributor's sample copy $1.

* Y.E.S. QUARTERLY, Young Entomologist's Society, Inc., 1915 Peggy Place, Lansing, MI 48910-2553. Gary A. Dunn, Editor. International journal of amateur entomology for older youth (junior and senior high) and adult amateurs interested in insects and spiders.

Publishes: Informative articles, essays, stories, and poems on insects and spiders. Black and white photos and line drawings are encouraged.

Submission Info: Manuscripts should be typed *single-spaced*. Photos must be in black and white. All drawings, maps, charts, etc. should be done in black ink and proportioned to fit journal's 5½" X 8½" size. Allow ½" margin all around. Whenever possible, state both common and scientific names for species mentioned in articles. Also, for the benefit of those living in other countries, identify state/province and country when giving locality information. Guidelines available in each issue or for SASE. Sample copy $1. No compensation given. Articles by members will be given priority, otherwise manuscripts are used on a first-come, first-serve basis. Receipt of all materials is acknowledged in writing.

Editor's Remarks: " *Y.E.S.* contains a wide variety of articles and information of interest to the amateur entomologist — tips for rearing and collecting insects, ideas for outdoor projects and experiments, field notes and checklists, tips for identifying insects, observations on insect behavior and habits, insects and computers, care of insect and spider collections, and more."

Subscription Rates: One year for nonmembers $25. For members $12. One year membership $6.

* YOUNG AMERICAN, AMERICA'S NEWSPAPER FOR KIDS, P.O. Box 12409, Portland, OR 97212. A monthly newspaper for kids ages 6 to 14, distributed as a supplement to metropolitan newspapers and directly to selected schools.

Publishes: Comics, jokes, puzzles, and opinion letters created by kids. Will also consider fiction manuscripts and "kid" news items.

Submission Info: Send complete work; no queries. News items should be 300 words or less, fiction should be 1,000 words or less. Send all material to the attention of: Kristina T. Linden, Editor. Be sure to include SASE with *all* submissions. Expect a response within six months after submission of manuscripts. Guidelines available for SASE. Sample issue $1.50.

Editor's Remarks: "A sample copy is the best guideline for writers. Children's writing that we receive is judged by the same standards we use in reading adult submissions, so it must be of high quality. We discourage 'classroom' assignments but welcome kids' comics, jokes, puzzles, and opinion letters."

* YOUNG AUTHOR'S MAGAZINE, 3015 Woodsdale Blvd., Lincoln, NE 68502-5053. An international classroom periodical for special, gifted, and talented young writers 6-19 years of age, published six times a year by Theraplan Inc., a nonprofit organization.

Publishes: Variety of material written and illustrated by young people ages 6-19, including cartoons, prose, and poetry.

Submission Info: Write to above address for information. Materials used are selected by volunteer reviewing editors, and are subject to change and copy editing. Sample copy $1.25.

Editor's Remarks: "*YAM* supports creative writing as a form of self-expression and self-improvement for all young people, regardless of mental or physical abilities."

Subscription Rates: Individual one year $9.95. Bulk classroom rates available. Note: A one year free subscription to *YAM* is included with membership to the National Association for Young Authors, an educational program also sponsored by Theraplan, Inc.

CHAPTER SEVEN
Understanding a Contest Listing

There are many different types of contests listed in this Guide. Some are sponsored through various publishers, some by individual artistic groups, and others by companies and associations. Contests are listed alphabetically except for those sponsored by on-line computer services, which are listed together in Chapter Nine.

Each listing contains three individual sections of information that will help you understand: (1) general information about the contest and its sponsor, (2) how entering the contest might benefit you, and (3) prize listings. There are also two optional sections. "Sponsor's Remarks" provides extra insight into the history or goals of the contest and/or advice for producing a winning entry. "Subscription Rates" has been included as an extra service for those interested in receiving a sponsor's publication on a regular basis.

Contests that are of special interest to young people are preceded with an asterisk (*). Contests that require an entry fee are marked with a dollar sign ($).

Information for each listing was provided directly from the contest sponsor and is as current as possible. Be sure to send for a complete list of current rules and requirements for each contest you wish to enter.

The following chart and sample contest listing will help explain the information contained within each section.

CONTEST LISTING CHART

SECTION	YOU WILL FIND	PAY SPECIAL ATTENTION TO
1	Name of Contest Mailing address for entries, forms, and complete list of rules. Brief description including who is eligible, frequency of contest. Name of sponsor.	Who sponsors this contest and the general theme of each contest. The goal of the contest.
2	General information about the contest. Deadlines for entries. Eligibility requirements. Entry fees, if any. How the contest is judged. Availability of rules and samples.	Any contest designed specifically for young people. Note any age limits. How to enter. Any restrictions.
3	Prizes awarded including cash, certificates, merchandise, and publication and display of winning entries.	The number of prizes awarded. How entries may be published or displayed. How often and how many times you may enter.
4	History of the contest, plus advice and tips for entering and winning, quoted directly from the sponsor or entry form.	Advice to help you submit a winning entry.
5	Subscription rates if sponsored by a publication. Subscription mailing address when it differs from contest entry address.	Included as an extra service for young people, parents, and teachers.

SAMPLE CONTEST LISTING

1 ——————— **CREATIVE KIDS,** GCT Inc., P.O. Box 6448, Mobile, AL 36660. A full size magazine by kids, for kids.

2 ——————— **General Info:** Various on-going and new contests. Examples: Goofy Gadgets (Rube Goldberg-type inventions drawn cartoon-style); Cover Photo Contest (candids of kids in action); Snap the Shutter; Cartoons; Artwork (submitted via slides or 35mm pictures. Open to children ages 5 to 18. Work must be nonviolent, nonsexist, and nonracist. All material must be labeled with the author's name, birthdate, home address, school name and school address. SASE with entry is required.

3 ——————— **Prizes:** Varies. Example: Winning cover photo entrants receive a one year free subscription; Goofy Gadget winner receives a four month subscription.

4 ——————— **Sponsor's Remarks:** "Creative Kids is the only award-winning, full size magazine with all of its contents contributed by gifted, creative, and talented youngsters. It includes children's work that represents their ideas, questions, fears, concerns, and pleasures. The prime purpose is to encourage children to strive for a product that is good enough for publication. It requires effort, discipline, and a sense of responsibility. The reward is to know that the material has appeared in print and is shared with thousands of readers."

5 ——————— **Subscription Rates:** One year $24. New reader rate for one year $17.97. Schools and libraries may request a free sample copy by sending a request on school or library stationery.

CHAPTER EIGHT
The Contest List

* AAA NATIONAL TRAFFIC SAFETY POSTER PROGRAM, Traffic Safety Department, 1000 AAA Drive, Heathrow, FL 32745. Annual program sponsored by the American Automobile Association for students K-12.

General Info: Open to any student enrolled in a public, parochial, or private elementary or secondary school, regardless of grade, who is less than 21 years of age before the deadline date. Overall poster size *must* be either 15" X 20" or 14" X 22" only, with a 3" space left at the bottom of the poster for the entry blank. Poster must be illustrated on the vertical axis only. Designs should be submitted on quality tag, poster, or illustration board or heavy paper. There is no limitation on the type of media – such as print, crayon, cut paper, felt pen, etc. – used on poster design; however, wood, plastic, glass, or metal should not be part of the poster. Designs may not incorporate any copyrighted characters, photographs, magazine, or newspaper illustrations. Other specific rules regarding design pertain to each of the four grade categories: primary (K-3); elementary (4-6); junior high (7-9); senior high (10-12). A AAA entry blank, or a reasonable facsimile, must be included. All designs must be the exclusive work of the student entering the program in idea, design, and execution. Completion of art should be done in school. All designs *must* illustrate only one of the two slogans assigned to their state and grade classification. Send for detailed rules and regulations, assigned slogans, and entry form.

Prizes: Savings bonds in varying amounts awarded to ten first, ten second, and ten third place winners within each grade category. Honorable Mention, Commendation, and Merit Citation certificates may also be awarded at the direction of the judges.

Sponsor's Remarks: "These posters, along with supplementary traffic safety educational materials, are distributed gratis to thousands of schools throughout the United States and Canada by local AAA clubs. More than six million reproductions of the winning poster designs are distributed annually."

*$ AMHAY MORGAN HORSE ART CONTEST, P.O. Box 960, Shelburne, VT 05482-0960. Annual contest sponsored by the American Morgan Horse Association. Open to both professional and amateur artists; special youth categories.

General Info: Beginning in 1990, there will be two judgings. The first will be divided into three age groups: 13 and under; 14-21, and Adult. The second judging will be divided into the three categories which are open to all ages. Three separate art categories: Morgan Art (including pencil sketches, oils, water colors, paintbrush, etc.); Morgan Cartoons; Morgan Specialty Pieces (sculptures, carvings, etc.). Enter as many times as you wish. Each entry must be accompanied by $2 entry fee and a completed entry form. All entries must be matted. *Unmatted artwork will not be considered in the judging.* Artwork must be original. It cannot be a copy of a photo that has been published unless the horse in the photo is the property of the artist. Submitted artwork becomes the property of the AMHA. Free contest rules and entry form available. Deadline for entries is December 1.

Prizes: Ribbons will be given to the top five places in the category judging. A ribbon and $50 will go to first place winner in each age category. Winning artworks will be displayed and auctioned at the annual AMHA Convention and will appear in *The Morgan Horse* magazine.

Sponsor's Remarks: "Works will be judged on creativity, artistic quality, breed promotion, and overall appearance. Selected works may be used for promotional purposes by the AMHA. When packaging artwork to mail, please be sure it is adequately protected. We cannot be responsible for work that is damaged in transport."

Subscription Rates: Write for rates for *The Morgan Horse.*

*$ AMHAY MORGAN HORSE PHOTOGRAPHY CONTEST, P.O. Box 960, Shelburne, VT 05482-0960. Annual contest sponsored by the American Morgan Horse Association. Open to both professional and amateur photographers; special youth category.

General Info: New theme for each year's contest. Two age categories: Junior (17 and under); Adult (18 and over). Theme for 1990 is "Morgans and Youth: Just for the Fun of It." Using the theme, submit a photograph containing a registered Morgan horse and provide caption. Photographs may be color or black and white prints, 5" X 7" or 8" X 10" in size. Mounting of photos is preferred but not required. A separate entry form must be used for each photo submitted; you may enter as many times as you wish. A $2 entry fee required for each photo submitted. A model release form for all identifiable people in the photo is also necessary. Entries must be postmarked by December 1. Complete rules, information, and entry form available free.

Prizes: Ribbons to six places and cash awards for the top two places in each age category. Cash awards are first place $50; second place $25. Prizes are awarded to the photographer, no matter who submits the photograph.

Sponsor's Remarks: "Photos will be judged on creativity, spontaneity of subject, technical quality, breed promotion, and overall appearance. Photos may be used for promotional purposes by AMHA and may be used in the AMHA Calendar, displayed at the Convention, or in *The Morgan Horse* magazine. Duplicates of the photograph may be used by the photographer."

Subscription Rates: Write for rates for *The Morgan Horse*.

*$ ARTS RECOGNITION AND TALENT SEARCH, National Foundation for Advancement of the Arts, 300 Northeast Second Avenue, Miami, FL 33132. Annual nonprofit program administered by the Miami-Dade Community College. Scholarship opportunities for high school students interested in dance, music, theatre, visual arts, and writing.

General Info: Contact your teacher, guidance counselor, or principal for complete registration packet. ARTS program is designed for high school seniors and other 17-18 year olds with demonstrable artistic achievements in dance, music, theatre, visual arts (including film and video), and writing. Application materials will also be sent to individuals by request. Fee of $25 for each discipline or discipline category entered; more for late entry.

Prizes: Winners receive between $500 and $3,000 in cash. NFAA earmarks up to $400,000 in cash awards for ARTS applicants whose work has been judged as outstanding by a national panel of experts. Selected candidates are also invited to Miami, Florida for a week of live adjudications [judging], consisting of auditions, master and technique classes, workshops, studio exercises, and interviews. NFAA pays travel, lodging, and meal expenses for the cash award candidates. Additional college scholarships and internships, worth over $3,000,000 have also been made available to all ARTS participants whether or not they were award winners.

Sponsor's Remarks: "ARTS is a unique program in that applicants are judged against a standard of excellence within each art discipline, not against each other. ARTS does not pre-determine the number of awards to be made on any level or in any discipline."

*$ BYLINE STUDENT CONTESTS, P.O. Box 130596, Edmond, OK 73013. Special contests for students during school year sponsored by *Byline* magazine, which is aimed at beginning writers.

General Info: Occasionally sponsors cartoon contests in addition to a variety of monthly writing contests for students 18 years and younger beginning with September issue and continuing through May each year. Most contests have a small entry fee that provides cash awards to winners. Other categories have no entry fee and are often used as class assignments by writing and English teachers. Send SASE for details of upcoming contests. Sample copy $3.

Prizes: Cash prizes and possible publication of students' manuscripts and cartoons.

Sponsor's Remarks: "*Byline* contests provide motivation for young writers/artists who enjoy winning cash awards, seeing their names and writing in print, and meeting deadlines."

Subscription Rates: One year (eleven issues) $18.

* **CREATIVE KIDS**, GCT Inc., P.O. Box 6448, Mobile, AL 36660. A full size magazine by kids, for kids.

General Info: Various on-going and new contests. Examples: Goofy Gadgets (Rube Goldberg-type inventions drawn cartoon-style); Cover Photo Contest (candids of kids in action); Snap the Shutter; Cartoons; Artwork (submitted via slides or 35mm pictures). Open to children ages 5 to 18. Work must be nonviolent, nonsexist, and nonracist. All material must be labeled with the author's name, birthdate, home address, school name, and school address. SASE with entry is required.

Prizes: Varies. Example: Winning cover photo entrants receive a one year free subscription; Goofy Gadget winner receives a four month subscription.

Sponsor's Remarks: "*Creative Kids* is the only award-winning, full size magazine with all of its contents contributed by gifted, creative, and talented youngsters. It includes children's work that represents their ideas, questions, fears, concerns, and pleasures. The prime purpose is to encourage children to strive for a product that is good enough for publication. It requires effort, discipline, and a sense of responsibility. The reward is to know that the material has appeared in print and is shared with thousands of readers."

Subscription Rates: One year $24. New reader rate for one year $17.97. Schools and libraries may request a free sample copy by sending a request on school or library stationery.

* **CRICKET LEAGUE CONTESTS**, P.O. Box 300, Peru, IL 61354. Monthly contests for children through age 14 sponsored by *Cricket* magazine.

General Info: Contest themes vary from month to month. Refer to a current issue of magazine. Throughout the year, contests are sponsored in four categories: art, poetry, short story, and photography. There are two age groups for each contest: 4-9 year olds and 10-14 year olds. All contest rules must be followed. Rules are listed in each issue. You must have your parent's or guardian's permission to send your entry. Each entry must be signed by your parent or guardian saying it is your own original work and that no help was given. Deadlines are the 25th of each month.

Prizes: Winners receive prizes or certificates and most place-winners' entries are published in the magazine.

Sponsor's Remarks: "We have no lower age limit, but 4 is the youngest entrant to date. The *Cricket* League has sponsored contests since the magazine's inception in September 1973. Through these contests, children have an opportunity to experience the rewards that creative writing and drawing bring. We receive an average of 300-800 entries per month, awarding twelve to twenty prizes and twenty to fifty honorable mentions."

Subscription Rates: Single copy $2.95. One year $22.97. Two year $49.97. Three years $69.97.

* **KIDSART/MAIL ART EXCHANGE,** P.O. Box 274, Mt. Shasta, CA 96067. Not a true competition, but a unique way to exchange art with kids around the world.

General Info: Ongoing "pen-pal" type exchange whereby a child decorates an envelope, front and back, with drawing, painting, stamps, stickers, cut and paste, etc. Child then mails decorated envelope to KidsArt with SASE (and letter, if desired) inside. KidsArt matches work with another entry and returns decorated art-envelopes to pen-pals in their SASEs. A detailed "rules" sheet with illustrations and suggestions is available for SASE. (Simplified, that means that your Art Envelope is sent to another kid, and someone else's Art Envelope is mailed back to you.) Note entries *must* include stamped, self-addressed envelope *inside* the decorated envelope. Without SASE, they are not able to mail back the "pen-pal's" art. There is no deadline. You may enter as often as you wish.

Prizes: The art-decorated pen-pal envelope you receive back is your prize. You may then write directly to your new pen pal if you wish.

Sponsor's Remarks: "KidsArt/Mail Art Exchange was started in spring of 1989. We exchange between 100 and 400 art envelopes each month. We try to match children by age and location (i.e. as far apart as possible). We do not match with other entries from their same school, club, or area. Infrequently this leads to a delay of one to two months before a match is possible. For example, if we get 500 entries from a school in Baltimore, it may take several weeks to get 500 matching entries from other parts of the country.

Subscription Rates: KidsArt publication available for one year, $8 for four issues.

* NATIONAL WRITTEN & ILLUSTRATED BY ... AWARDS CONTEST FOR STUDENTS, Landmark Editions, Inc., 1402 Kansas Avenue, Kansas City, MO 64127. Annual book contest for students. Books are sold to schools, libraries. May also be purchased through bookstores, at educational conventions, and by direct mail.

General Info: Original books may be entered in *one* of three age categories: 6-9, 10-13, and 14-19 years of age. Each book must be written and illustrated by the same student. Send a self-addressed business-size (#10) envelope, with 50¢ postage to receive complete contest rules and guidelines.

Prizes: Winners receive all-expense-paid trips to Landmark's offices in Kansas City, where editors and art directors assist them in the final preparation of text and illustrations for the publication of their books. Winners also receive publishing contracts and are paid royalties. In addition, the winners and four runners-up in each of the three age categories receive college scholarships from the R.D. and Joan Dale Hubbard Foundation, amounting to: Each winner $5,000; each second place $2,000; each third, fourth, and fifth places $1,000.

Sponsor's Remarks: "Contest sponsored to encourage and cele-brate the creative efforts of students. Every year students nation-wide submit more than 4,500 original book entries. The winning books are selected by a national panel of distinguished educators, editors, art directors, and noted authors and illustrators of juvenile books."

* NEWSCURRENTS STUDENT EDITORIAL CARTOON CON-TEST, P.O. Box 52, Madison, WI 53701. (800) 356-2303. Sponsored by Knowledge Unlimited, Inc., *NewsCurrents* is a weekly current events discussion program for students in grades 3 to 12. Contest held annually since 1989, with approximately 10,000 entries sub-mitted each year.

General Info: Entrants must submit original cartoons on any sub-ject of national or international interest. Students may submit as many cartoons as they wish. Open to all elementary, middle, or high school students K-12. Use black ink on white paper, and draw and letter in bold lines. If possible, draw your cartoon in a slightly horizontal format. Print your name, your teacher's name, grade, school, city, and state on the back of the cartoon. Select news sto-ries of major continuing interest for your cartoons. Don't 'clutter' it with too many different ideas. Be original. While your cartoon may express a widely held view of a leader or issue, it should not reflect another cartoonist's way of expressing that idea. Cartoons will be judged primarily on the basis of originality, clarity, and knowledge of the subject. The artistic merit of the cartoon will be considered secondarily. Submitted cartoons cannot be returned. Detailed guidelines available.

Prizes: Each first place winner in each of three grade categories (K-6; 7-9; 10-12) receives a $100 savings bond. Each second place winner receives $75 savings bond. Each third place winner receives a $50 savings bond. Honorable mention certificates will go to oth-ers whose cartoons deserve special recognition. All winning car-toons will appear in *NewsCurrents* and will be publicized in other ways. The top 100 entries are published in a book, *Editorial Car-toons By Kids.*

Sponsor's Remarks: "We hear so much about how ignorant and apathetic American young people are ... well, the outpouring of entries for this contest gives us reason to believe otherwise. As these editorial cartoons show, kids care *very much* about their world – the environment, poverty, hunger, drugs, the deficit, and so on. And these young people have proven that when given the right educational tools and opportunities, they are capable of a high level of critical thought and understanding, as well as concern."

Subscription Rates: Write or call for rates.

*$ QUILL AND SCROLL NATIONAL WRITING/PHOTOGRA-PHY CONTEST, *Quill and Scroll*, School of Journalism, University of Iowa, Iowa City, IA 52242. Contest open to grades 9 to 12.

General Info: Competition open to all high school students – *Quill & Scroll* membership is not required. Each school may submit two entries in ten categories: editorial, editorial cartoon, investigative reporting (individual and team), news story, feature story, sports story, advertisement, and photography (news feature and sports). Entry fee of $1 per entry must accompany each entry. Contest rules are sent, in late December, to all schools on mailing list. Guidelines and entry form also appear in the Dec./Jan. issue of *Quill & Scroll* magazine. If your school does not receive information about this contest, request information from the above address. Materials will be sent to the journalism advisor, principal, or counselors at our school. See contest guidelines sheet for format and detailed information for each category. NOTE: Senior national winners are automatically eligible for the Edward J. Nell Memorial Scholarship in Journalism.

Prizes: National winners will be notified by mail through their advisors and receive the Gold Key Award, and be listed in April/May issue *Quill & Scroll*. Senior winners with intent to major in journalism at a college or university that offers a major in journalism are eligible for a $500 scholarship.

Sponsor's Remarks: "Currently enrolled high school students are invited to enter the National Writing/Photo Contest. Awards are made in each of the ten divisions.

*$ QUILL AND SCROLL YEARBOOK EXCELLENCE CON-TEST, Quill and Scroll Society, School of Journalism, University of Iowa, Iowa City, IA 52242.

General Info: Contest is open to students in grades 9-12. Students must attend a high school that is chartered by Quill and Scroll (more than 10,000 schools are chartered). Each school may submit two spread sheet entries in each of eleven categories. These are: student life, academics, sports action photo, academic photo, feature photo, graphic, and index. Only one entry may be submitted for the Theme Development division. (Twelve divisions.) Submit $1.50 entry fee for each division, $34.50 maximum. Entry applications will be sent to each member school in late August. You may request applications or membership information from the above address.

Prizes: Winners receive a Gold Key Award and are eligible to apply for the Edward J. Nell scholarship during their senior year.

Sponsor's Remarks: "We will offer this contest for the fourth year this fall 1990."

* REFLECTIONS CULTURAL ARTS PROGRAM, The National PTA, 700 North Rush Street, Chicago, IL 60611. Annual program sponsored and conducted by the National Parent/Teacher Association.

General Info: The "Reflections" program has three parts: the program and the theme search, which are both open to all students who attend a school where there is a PTA/PTSA in good standing, and the scholarship program, which is available to all high school seniors who enter the "Reflections" program during 1990-1991. (See current guidelines for later years.) All the necessary forms and rules needed to participate are available through the above address. Note, you must enter the program through your local registered PTA/PTSA chapter. The 1990-91 theme is "If I Had A Wish." Entries accepted in the following categories: literature, music, photography, and visual arts. Categories are also divided into four grade levels: primary, intermediate, junior high, and high school. Visual arts accepted are: printmaking, including all graphic processes – linoleum cuts, serigraphs, wood cuts, computer-generated art, or vegetable prints; drawing – crayon, chalk, charcoal, pencil, ink, or any other medium used for drawing and sketching; collage; and needlework. Visual art rules allow only two-dimensional artwork on paper, poster board, or canvas. Sculpture, ceramics, jewelry, or other three-dimensional arts and crafts are not eligible for entry. Entries must be received in the national PTA office by April 5, 1991, accompanied by the official entry form. Late entries will be disqualified.

Prizes: Outstanding interpretation winners receive an expense-paid trip to the National PTA Convention, a $250 scholarship awarded by QSP, Inc., the fundraising subsidiary of *Reader's Digest*, and a gold-plated "Reflections" medallion. Other substantial cash and gifts (such as encyclopedias) are also awarded in each grade category and each interpretation category.

Sponsor's Remarks: "Students' interpretation of the theme is endless. For example, a child might wish for a pony, a new bike, happiness or world peace. The list is endless! This theme will allow the children to use their creativity, so encourage them to explore their thoughts and feelings."

* SCHOLASTIC AWARDS, 730 Broadway, New York, NY 10003. Annually sponsored programs for writing, art, and photography for students in grades 7-12.

General Info: Scholastic Writing Awards include classifications covering fiction, nonfiction, poetry, and drama. Scholastic Art Awards cover the fields of painting, drawing, printmaking, design, sculpture, and crafts. Scholastic Photography Awards have divisions for both black and white, and color. Complete information appears in individual rule books for *each* of the divisions, available between October 1 and January 1. When requesting rule books, please send postcard and specify book needed (writing, art, or photography) to above address.

Prizes: Writing Awards include cash prizes and certificates of merit. Smith-Corona also offers honor awards of portable typewriters. In addition, scholarship awards are offered by Smith-Corona, National Broadcasting Co., M.R. Robinson Fund, and the Tisch School of the Arts, New York University. See rules books for awards given for art and photography.

Sponsor's Remarks: "For sixty-four years, the Scholastic Awards program has recognized creative achievements in grades 7-12 in schools across the United States, Canada, and U.S. schools abroad. An estimated 250,000 entries are submitted annually in the three divisions."

* TIME EDUCATION PROGRAM STUDENT ART COMPETITION, Communications Park, Box 8000, Mount Kisco, NY 10549. Annual art competition for high school students sponsored by *Time* Education Program.

General Info: High schools in the U.S. and Canada are eligible, but each student must be sponsored by a teacher. Students may enter one original two-dimensional art piece (no larger than 11" X 17") in *one* of the following categories, which correspond to *Time*: (1) *Time* cover design, including logo and red border; (2) political cartoon; (3) maps, charts, or graphs. Send SASE for more information and the required entry form.

Prizes: Three first prizes of $1,000 awarded. Three second prizes of $500 awarded.

Sponsor's Remarks: "This (1991) will be the 11th annual writing contest sponsored by T.E.P *Timelines*, a publication of the Time Education Program."

Subscription Rates: *Time* is available at newsstands, at stores, and by subscription.

* YOUNG PEOPLE'S FILM & VIDEO FESTIVAL, 1219 S.W. Park Avenue, Portland, OR 97205. Annual competition sponsored by the Northwest Film & Video Center, a division of the Oregon Arts Institute. Other sponsors and grants help support the project.

General Info: Open to any film or video maker from kindergarten through college living in Oregon, Washington, Idaho, Montana, or Alaska. Panel of judges selects winning works in five grade categories: K-3, 4-6, 7-9, 10-12, and college/university. All entries must be student-produced. Send SASE for detailed rules, guidelines, and yearly deadlines.

Prizes: Winning works will be shown at an awards ceremony during the Festival. They will later be broadcast on public television.

Sponsor's Remarks: "You may call (503) 221-1156 for complete information and exact Festival dates. Many entries each year are from classes or other student groups working together. This is something we highly encourage and recommend due to the number of 'jobs' involved in producing a quality film or video."

CHAPTER NINE
On-line Markets & Contests

As the number of computer information services such as CompuServe and GEnie grow, so too will the number and variety of marketing and contest opportunities for young people. Already there are several dozen special interest groups (SIGs) on each service waiting for communication questions and messages, as well as files (manuscripts) to add to various on-line libraries.

In anticipation of the third edition of *Market Guide for Young Writers* and this new *Market Guide for Young Artists and Photographers,* a number of SIGs were contacted directly (via personal computer and modem) and asked whether they would welcome more participation from young people aged eighteen and under. The response was a unanimous "YES!" not only from the forum administrators (more commonly known as SYSOPS), but from many individual computer services members who took time to reply.

It was not possible for us to contact each and every one of the various SIGs. However, below you will find a sampling of various groups of particular interest to young writers, which are easily found on either CompuServe Information Services or the General Electric network service, GEnie. Similar groups might also be found on other information services such as Prodigy. If you have a special hobby or interest (virtually anything from aquariums to zoology, casual or technically-oriented) be sure to check in the information service directory, which comes with your membership, for additional forums, roundtables, and SIGs in which to participate.

To locate appropriate markets for your work, it's best to check the descriptions of the various sections (or categories) and libraries within individual SIGs. For instance, in the Writers' Ink roundtable on GEnie, poems on a variety of topics are most appropriate within Category 3 "The Poet's Corner." Individual section subjects include: "The Playroom," which features humorous poems, "The Nursery" with poems for children, and "Refrigerator Door," which features poems by children. While there is also a section called "The Hidden Room" for science fiction-related poems and messages by SFPA members, GEnie also has a separate roundtable devoted just to discussions about science fiction and fantasy. Plus, you could even join the writers' workshop there.

On CompuServe, section 9 in the Pets/Animal Forum is reserved for favorite pet stories, while members upload pet-related computer graphics into section 12. The Students' Forum is most popular with middle school students who like to share their ideas and interests with other students around the country. (It's a popular meeting place for middle school teachers, too.) Section 8 features original compositions and poems, as well as related "conversations" (in the form of messages) from members to other members and between members and the SYSOPs. Section 12 is designated the Pen-Pals area, and student art is featured in section 13.

News about on-line writing, art, and photography contests are often featured in special messages that scroll by when you first log on. To access the specific rules and regulations of each contest, you need to go into the SIG that is sponsoring the contest and download the special library file containing the information. If you don't know where to look, post a message to a SYSOP and one will reply within a day or two.

On-line Guidelines

Basically, most of the guidelines for preparing traditional manuscripts and art apply equally well to on-line markets and contests. That means spending time writing, rewriting, revising, and polishing your stories; checking for grammar, spelling, and punctuation mistakes; and making sure you are submitting an appropriate manuscript. (For instance, a personal experience story about your pet alligator may be more welcome in the Pet Forum on CompuServe than in the Literary Forum, though it might be equally welcome in the Students' Forum.)

In addition, remember that most library files must be sent (uploaded) in standard ASCII code or as a binary file using a file transfer protocol such as XMODEM. Also check the specific requirements of each SIG before uploading graphic arts and photography.

Again, ask the SYSOPS for advice about which type of graphic format to use, as well as which protocol to use while uploading. Don't be shy about asking questions. SYSOPS, like Jack Smith (Writers' Ink on GEnie), Mike Wilmer (Photography Forum on CompuServe), and Larry Wood (Computer Art and Graphics Forums on CompuServe) all agree that the only dumb questions are the ones that aren't asked!

While there are rarely, if ever, any additional costs involved with becoming a member of an individual SIG, you must become a subscriber of the service before you can participate. Young people are allowed to access the services by using someone else's identification number and password, such as a parent, school class, or friend, as long as they receive permission *from that person or group* before they log on. In addition, regular "connect" charges (based on a standard hourly rate) do apply while you are posting messages, participating in a workshop or real-time conference, or downloading library files. The amount of these charges varies depending on which service you have subscribed to. In many ways, these connect charges are similar to subscribing to a magazine and the paper, postage, and envelope costs you would normally pay in order to submit to traditional markets and contests, except that the cost is higher. One good point to remember is that most times, connect fees are *not* charged while you are uploading manuscripts or graphic files into a SIG library. Long-distance charges are something else to consider if you don't have a local access number to your particular service.

You'll also need to check for the proper software and protocol formats to use when accessing educational computer services, such as the AT&T Learning Network and BreadNet. Some services will provide the correct software needed when you sign up.

Creative Computing

A major benefit to accessing on-line marketing opportunities is the unique creativity displayed and encouraged by those participating. For instance, because time *is* money on-line, the messages members post are usually brief and informal. However, by incorporating acronyms and "emoticons," these messages are often laced with emotion and humor, as well as information.

Acronyms are letters used in place of full words. Examples frequently seen on-line are: **BTW** − by the way; **OTOH** − on the other hand; **OIC** − Oh, I see!; **GR8** − that's great; and **g,d&r** − grinning, ducking, and running. These last examples and other words such as **<grin>**, **<blush>**, and **<chuckle>** are used to make sure the other person knows when you're teasing or making a joke.

Emoticons are icons (characters such as punctuation marks and letters) which designate emotion most often by the way they resemble a person's face. (Note: In order to "read" an emoticon, you have to tilt your head and look sideways at the picture.) Common emoticons are: :) − a smiley face; :(− a sad face; =:O − surprise; :P − smiley face with tongue sticking out. Here are a few more examples: &:-) − message from a person with wavy hair; (O--< − a "fishy" message; @>--->---- − a rose for someone special.

Another benefit available on-line is the potential to share information and to get critiques on your work relatively quickly rather than waiting days, weeks, or even months for a reply to come through the postal service. (No wonder computer buffs call regular mail "snail mail"!) Plus, you will often have the chance to correspond directly with publishers, editors, agents, and professional writers, artists, and photographers. This sort of opportunity occurs most often during a "real-time" conference sponsored by a special interest group.

On-line Market and Contest List

AT&T LEARNING NETWORK, P.O. Box 45155, Jacksonville, FL 32232-9897. A curriculum-based program that links together a community of educators and students using AT&T worldwide telecommunications network. Classrooms are joined together electronically with groups of geographically distant peers who benefit from cooperative efforts to achieve their educational goals. Choice of six curriculum areas offered: Computer Chronicles, Mind Works, Places and Perspectives, Energy Works, Society's Problems, and Global Issues. Young people must participate through their school. Write for detailed program subscription kit.

BREADNET, c/o William W. Wright, Jr., Director of Information, Bread Loaf School of English, Middlebury College, Middlebury, VT 05733. A curriculum-based computer communication network that encourages young writers. Program includes: advice for brainstorming ideas, interviewing techniques, and collaborative writing; pointers on collecting and distributing writing shared by participating students; encouragement for peer-critiquing among students; and more. Write for complete details.

(Note: Send SASE to *The Writing Notebook*, P.O. Box 1268, Eugene, OR 97440-1268, for a list of additional education-related computer programs and projects.)

COMPUSERVE INFORMATION SERVICES, P.O. Box 20212, 5000 Arlington Centre Blvd., Columbus, OH 43220. A computer information service featuring a variety of special interest forums open to member subscribers. Many forums sponsor periodic contests. Prizes vary but sometimes include gifts such as a camera lens, free film, prominent display of art or manuscripts in library file, and/or free access time on the service. Forums of special interest to young writers, artists, and photographers include:

Art Gallery Forum (GO GALLERY) – Upload pictures you have drawn by hand or on computer; also view computer-image pictures of famous paintings, and scenic locations. Subjects range from portraits to panoramas to posters.

Aquaria and Fish (GO FISHNET) – Get and give advice about building, managing, and stocking aquariums; share "fish" stories, both fiction and nonfiction.

Computer Art & Graphics Forums (GO COMART or GO PICS) – Download artworks, digitalized photographs, and scanned images (often of original art and photos) uploaded by others, as well as upload your own. Separate sections include: people and portraits; animal kingdom, nature, fantasy, and science fiction; cartoons and comics; cars, boats, and planes. Hall of Fame section includes contest winners and other selected works, including that created by young people of special interest and/or that demonstrates effort and talent. Uses GIF format. For viewing GIF images, a decoder is available in the PICS Forum, library 3.

Journalism Forum (GO JFORUM) – Most members are (or want to be) professional journalists. Has separate sections and libraries for those interested in radio, TV, print media (such as magazines and newspapers), and photo/video journalists.

Literary Forum (GO LITFORUM) — Gathering place for professional writers, literature readers, journalists, humorists, and those with an interest in related fields. Sections include poetry and lyrics, controversial topics, fiction discussions, science fiction, comics and humor, stage and screen, nonfiction and technical. Separate section for writers of children's material as well as material written by young writers.

Motor Sports Forum (GO RACING) — Provides opportunities to have related material read by the "top folks in the business." Young people welcome.

Outdoors Forum (GO OUTDOORS) — Contains many interesting articles by members of the Outdoor Writers Association. Young people are welcome to contribute. Sections include: outdoor photography, fishing, hunting, cycle/run/walk, water sports, snow sports, firearms, environment.

Pets/Animals Forum (GO PETS) — Special section for "My Favorite Pet" stories, fiction or nonfiction, also articles, tips, and advice for owners of various types of pets.

Photography Forum (GO PHOTOFORUM) — Sections include digital imaging, black and white or color film, photo news and issues, shooting techniques. Sponsors special photo contest with two categories: professional and amateur. Open to young people twelve and older. Contest entries are judged on-line by professionals in the field. Entries may be uploaded directly to the forum if you have the necessary equipment, or send photos by U.S. mail and they will be "digitalized" for you for free.

Students' Forum (GO STUFO) — Popular with middle school students who share their ideas and interests with other students around the country. Sections on many topics including original compositions and poetry, pen pals, and student art. STUFO member list available in library 2, which includes names, ID's, and the schools each attends.

GENIE, 401 N. Washington Street, Rockville, MD 20850. A computer information service featuring a variety of special interest roundtables open to member subscribers. Announcements of upcoming special events such as real-time conferences and contests appear on a banner each time you log on. However, you will need to move into individual roundtables (RT) for information about additional opportunities. Of special interest to young people:

Genealogy RT (GENEALOGY) – Primary goal is to stimulate people to exchange genealogical information, whether it is about specific family members, about primary sources available, or about other means of gathering or exchanging information.

Hobby RT (HOBBYRT) – Within the separate categories are topics on almost any hobby including trains, planes, doll houses, card collecting, etc. Members are welcome to share information about their favorite subjects.

Maggie-Mae's Pet-Net & Co RT (PET) – Goal is to help animals, pet owners, and animal lovers to lead happier, healthier lives. Members share important and interesting information about animals, as well as related topics just for fun and enjoyment.

Photography RT (PHOTO) – For both professional and amateur photographers.

Science Fiction and Fantasy RT (SFRT) – Devoted to discussion of science fiction, fantasy, horror, and other related areas in all their forms (writing, movies, TV, cartoons, comics, etc.). Sponsors a writers' workshop and regular meetings with members, plus famous individuals from various fields often stop by to field questions and offer advice.

TeleJoke RT (JOKE) – Section contains the best jokes submitted from over 65,000 regular readers around the world at a rate of two to five added per day. This is the place to interact with other GEnie "funny" people.

Writers' Ink (M 440) – Electronic writer's group that welcomes and encourages participation by young people. Members range from beginners to seasoned professionals including journalists, poets, and novelists. Has active discussion area. Members may upload manuscripts to special category sections. Topics cover all types of writing including lyrics. Holds periodical contests for writers.

PRODIGY SERVICES COMPANY, 445 Hamilton Avenue, White Plains, NY 10601. A computer information service featuring a variety of special interest groups open to member subscribers. Contact directly for information about on-line membership and opportunities.

CHAPTER TEN

Answers to Questions Young Artists & Photographers Ask

How do I know how many pictures to include with my story?

Start by studying how many and what kind of pictures are included in the markets you would like to submit to. Obviously, a magazine may only need one or two pictures to go with a story, while a picture book will need one for almost every page.

What is a model release form?

Sometimes a publication or contest will ask the submitter to provide a statement, signed by the person granting an interview or identified in an artwork or a photograph, to prove that he or she agreed to being interviewed, photographed, painted, or otherwise represented. You can make your own model release form using a clean sheet of paper containing your name, address, and phone number, and the name, address, phone number of the person being interviewed, photographed, or used as a model. Have that person write a sentence or two that clearly shows he or she understands that the information or work may be used by you and possibly be published. Then have that person sign his or her name and the date. You or someone else should sign it as a witness, too. (Sample model release forms may be found in professional publications such as *The Artist's Market*, or *Professional Business Practices in Photography*. See Appendix Two.)

Most people don't mind providing this information. If you are creating something about someone eighteen or younger, have their parent or guardian also sign the model release form.

Where can I find help making films and videos?

Beginning filmmakers can often find how-to help as well as outlets for their work by contacting community recreation centers, local, regional, or state art councils, and community colleges. If there are no classes specifically for a young person, ask for permission to enroll in an "adult" class. If film and video making aren't offered, try a still photography class to learn about composition, contrast, and lighting. And a dramatic writing or acting class will help you learn other aspects of production. Maybe you will meet people who will want to work with you on a project.

If there are no local markets or contests for your work, ask for new categories to be included, or sponsor a contest of your own.

What should I put in my portfolio?

Since a portfolio is used as a showcase for your work, you want to make sure it represents the best work you can do. The actual number of pieces isn't as important as *what* you include. A selection of your work sent to a magazine may only include three to six pieces of work, but they may all be *photocopies* of pen and ink drawings because that is the medium the magazine accepts. (Note: you wouldn't send them in a portfolio case.) On the other hand, you should include ten to fifteen pieces of your best work in a variety of mediums if you are going to be showing it to galleries and book publishers. Professional book illustrators often include a book dummy using a familiar fairy or folk tale to show how they would illustrate the story. Always make sure to include at least one piece of "finished" artwork.

Do all writers and artists need an agent? How do I hire one?

No, you do not need an agent, particularly if you are still in school. Many professional writers and artists submit their work directly to a publisher without using an agent. Most agents only handle book contracts from people who have published before. There are several reference books for writers and artists that give information about finding an agent.

Why should I include a SASE?

SASE is the abbreviation for self-addressed stamped envelope. All editors and most contests insist that people submitting material include a SASE with their work. The editor will use it to send you an answer, or to return your work to you if it is rejected. To prepare a SASE, write *your* name and address on the front of an envelope as if you were mailing it to yourself. Be sure to put enough postage on your SASE, usually the same amount that you put on your mailing envelope. (*Example*: If it costs you $1.25 to mail your illustrations and manuscript, you must also put $1.25 postage on your SASE.) Put your SASE inside the mailing envelope with the rest of your submission.

I sent a self-addressed stamped envelope with my work but I never received a reply. What should I do?

It often takes an editor four to eight weeks to respond. If you have waited this long, send a polite letter to the editor asking if he received your package and if he has made a decision. Be sure to include another SASE (it can be a regular business-size envelope with appropriate postage or (IRC) or self-addressed stamped postcard. Some markets receive so much mail that they cannot respond to it all. Check the listings and guideline sheets. If a market says, "Does not respond" or "Does not return submissions" you do not have to enclose a SASE. And you may not hear from them if your work is rejected. However, if you want to make sure an editor or contest has received your package, enclose a postage-paid *postcard* addressed to you. On the note side write the title or description of your submission, the date you mailed it, and your name and address. Draw a line for the editor to mark the date it was received.

If you still receive no answer from a market that normally responds and returns work, write again asking the editor to return your package. If another three weeks pass with no response, prepare a new packet of your work and send it to another market. You should remember also to keep copies of your artwork, or the negative from a photo, so you can redo those too.

Most editors try to be as prompt as possible.

Can I send material to a publication or contest that is not listed in *Market Guide for Young Artists & Photographers*?

For various reasons, not all publications that consider material created by young people are listed in this Guide. Some editors have asked not to be listed because they prefer that only their readers submit material. If you have read a notice in a publication asking for submissions, you are considered a reader and may send them your submission whether or not they are listed in this Guide. Be careful to follow their guidelines. A few markets and contests restrict entries to subscribers or members of a particular organization, or some other criteria.

There may be other publications we were not aware of, or were too new at the time this edition was printed, that may also consider your work. (*If you discover a market or contest not listed in this edition, please send us their name and address so we may contact them for possible inclusion in future editions. Also let us know if you experience any problems submitting to one of the markets or contests listed.*)

Can I send the same work to more than one magazine at the same time?

Most often this refers to manuscripts rather than artwork and photographs. However, the answer is the same for each. Sending the same work to more than one market at the same time is called "simultaneous submission." It is not recommended for either adults or young people. However, you may send different work to separate publications at the same time. Be sure to keep a record of which material you sent to which market.

Most contests want only new material that has not been submitted to another contest or market before.

Why does a listing say "send holiday or seasonal material six months in advance"?

It takes the entire publication staff several months to collect, edit, and print a single issue. Therefore, they must consider material several months in advance of the issue's scheduled appearance. Often editors are reading Christmas stories in July and surfing stories in December. This is called the "lead time." Different publications have different lead times. Generally, the lead time for a book is longer than a magazine. And a magazine's lead time is much longer than the lead time for a newspaper.

What is an International Reply Coupon?

United States postage cannot be used by publications in other countries, including Canada, to mail a letter or your work back to you. (This is true for other countries, too. For instance, Canadians need to include an IRC when submitting to a U.S. address.) If you wish to submit to a foreign market, ask a postal clerk for an International Reply Coupon to enclose with your self-addressed envelope instead of a regular postage stamp. The editor will exchange the International Reply Coupon (IRC) for proper postage.

Can my friend and I send in a story we wrote and illustrated together?

Certainly. Be sure to put both your names and addresses (and any other information required) on the material.

Can I submit pictures I've drawn featuring my favorite cartoon characters?

Like written work, illustrations and photographs are protected by copyright, and sometimes trademarks, too. Most of the time, markets and contests will want you to submit material that is *completely* original. That means that you not only created the picture or cartoon, but created the characters all on your own. *Occasionally*, there may be times when you can submit new pictures featuring someone else's characters. (Remember, your classmate's work is protected by the same copyright laws that protect famous people's work!) One example is in the computer field where you may create computer graphic images of favorite cartoon characters and upload them onto an on-line service. This is more a display of your computer talent rather than your talent as an artist.

It is always best (and more rewarding!) to create something yourself from scratch.

And never be tempted to say you created something original when you didn't. That's plagiarism, and it's against the law. Just imagine how *you'd* feel if someone took credit for something you made!

My work won first place in a contest. Can I send it to a magazine to be printed too?

Some contests retain the copyright to entries and some do not. It should state in the rules whether you may submit your work elsewhere. If the rules are not clear, write the sponsor requesting an answer. Be sure to include your name and address, the contest you entered, the title of your piece, and what awards you have won. If you do submit it elsewhere be sure to tell that market that it was previously submitted and if it was published, when it appeared and who published it.

Do I have to subscribe to a magazine before I can send them my work?

It depends. Some magazines want material only from their current readers. Two of these are *Odyssey* and *Touch*. Readers will find submission guidelines in current issues. If you don't have the magazines delivered to your home but read it in your school, library, or church, some magazines still consider you a reader and you may submit material. However, for most markets you do not need to subscribe before you submit material.

Do the manuscripts I send with my work *have* to be typed? I don't own a typewriter or computer. What can I do?

Some editors will accept handwritten manuscripts if they are neat and easy to read. Most markets for teens, however, require manuscripts to be typed. Try borrowing or renting a typewriter, or find someone who will type it for you. Many schools and libraries have typewriters you can use.

My friend said I had to register my photographs before I can have them published. Is this true, and how do I do it?

Your friend is referring to registering a copyright. Your photographs (artwork and manuscripts, too) are automatically protected by copyright law the moment you create them. (That generally means you have put it in some form that can be shared, which includes film negatives.) Ideas (especially ones still just in your head!) and titles aren't protected by copyright. You do not need to register a copyright before submitting photographs, or other work, to markets or contests.

For more complete information about copyrights write to: United States Copyright Office, Library of Congress, Washington, DC 20599. The information is free. Laws may differ in other countries.

Do I have to cash the check I got from a magazine? I want to frame it.

By all means, cash it. Consider framing a copy of your published piece instead. You might also consider framing a photocopy of the check or a single dollar bill along with your check stub to signify your first "for pay" sale.

What is a "theme list"?

Some magazines plan monthly issues around a certain topic or theme, such as medicine, sports heroes, dating, etc. Most market listings will specify if a publication follows a theme list. You may write for a list of upcoming themes. (Include SASE.) The deadline dates for submitting material will be included to help you meet their lead time.

I'm confused. Do I send my original work and keep a copy or do I send the copy and keep my original?

This is a hard question to answer. In some cases, you would send your original artwork (carefully packaged) and keep a photocopy. You would also send developed photos or slides rather than the negatives. However, there are many contests (only a few are listed here) that insist or prefer that a slide picture of your work be entered for judging rather than the original work. Refer to guideline sheets for the correct format in which to submit. For advice on how to photograph your art (whatever medium) consult *Photographing Your Art*. (See Appendix Two for publisher and address.)

However, many markets actually prefer that you submit clear photocopies of your work because they worry about protecting the condition of your original pieces. If they like your work, they will request that you send the originals. If you aren't sure what to send, or would be upset if something happened to your originals, send photocopies first.

What should I do with material that is rejected?

First of all, try hard not to take it personally. There are many reasons work is rejected and some have nothing to do with how well, or poorly, it was done. Look for another market or contest to submit it to. The key is to keep trying.

What does "copyright" mean?

For writers, artists, and photographers "copy" means their creative work. "Right" refers to the person who has the authority to sell a certain piece of written, drawn, or photographed work. When you create something, you automatically become the copyright owner by law. If an editor agrees to publish your work, he will "buy the rights" to it. There are various rights you may grant an editor or a contest. Generally, magazines buy "one-time rights" which gives them permission to print your work one time. Then the rights are returned to you and you may offer the same work to another editor for "second" or "reprint" rights. A number of publications and contests buy "all rights" which means that once you agree the publication can print your work, or you enter it into a contest, it becomes their property and is no longer yours. You may not send it to another market. Note that "buys" does not always mean that you will receive payment in exchange for giving your permission to publish your work.

Most articles published in newspapers enter what is known as "public domain" and may be reprinted, or the information used, by anyone, though credit is usually given to the original source. Sometimes you will see a copyright notice on a newspaper article that is of special importance or on a subject of great interest. The copyright notice protects that particular work from being reused without written permission. There may be times when you'll want to include a copyright notice to protect your work, such as when you don't want a cartoon that is to be published in a newsletter to enter public domain, or you have published your own book. Include a copyright notice too, when you create your own written and illustrated books. Remember, however, that you do not have to officially register a copyright (and pay a fee) before you can put a copyright notice on your work.

Copyrights can be very confusing. For more information about current copyright laws and a free list of other government brochures write to: United States Copyright Office, Library of Congress, Washington, DC 20599.

Computer-related Questions

My teacher has tried to upload some of our stories in the Literary Forum on CompuServe but we can never find them listed in the library section. Where are they?

Literary Forum SYSOP Janet McConnaughey says that people uploading files often forget to include line feeds or carriage returns at the end of *each* line of text. That means you need to press "ENTER" or "RETURN" as *each* line of type gets to the edge of the screen. Most word processors automatically wrap words that go beyond the screen to the next line. However, you'll need to do this manually for manuscripts you want to upload. Just remember to type as if you were using an older-style typewriter — the kind with a handle that sticks out the right side, which you push to make the platen advance one line and return to the left margin.

(Check individual on-line systems for the maximum number of

characters that can be included in one line of type. This is sometimes referred to as "number of columns." A typical width is eighty
columns.)

For additional help, check both your word processing software
manual and the manual that explains how to use your modem
communications software.

**Do I need my own user ID number and password to log onto a
computer system like CompuServe or GEnie?**

Generally, students within a classroom or school, as well as family
members, may share one user ID number and password. However,
the subscription will only be registered under one name. On GE-
nie, users may use nicknames to sign messages. CompuServe prefers that users always use their regular names. Before you log on,
make sure you have permission. You might want to sign messages
and identify files with your own name, then add the name of the
person who has the subscription. Example: John (Joe Smith's son).

How can I tell what stories are written by kids?

Sometimes you can't, unless the manuscript was uploaded as part
of a contest that had special categories for different ages. Young
writers who want their ages known can add the information to the
uploaded file, in the file description, or in the keywords area.

If you're looking for files written by kids, look for addresses
within the files or descriptions that indicate a school or class. Example: Written by students at Perry Middle School.

**I'm having trouble uploading and downloading files. Where do I
get help?**

First make sure you've read your user's manuals. If a parent or
teacher can't help you, leave a message to the SYSOP in the special interest group (SIG) you're trying to access. You might also try
asking for help at your local computer store. Also, many software
manufacturers and on-line information systems have toll-free 800
numbers you can call to talk to a real person.

Is there any way to save on connect charges when I want to log onto a computer information service?

There are several software packages that can help you "automate" your sessions by allowing you to log on, go straight to the SIG you want, automatically up or download a file, then log off all with the push of one or two keys. These are often referred to as "navigation" programs.

Several are available for CompuServe users, including ATOSIG, and TAPICS for MS-DOS users (IBM & compatible systems), CompuServe's Information Manager, Navigator for the Macintosh, ST/FORUM for the Atari ST, and WHAP! for Amiga users. GEnie users with IBM or IBM compatible systems can use Aladdin. (A version for Apples and the Macintosh systems is under development.) Most of these software programs can be downloaded and tried free on a trial basis directly from the computer service. Note, you pay connect charges while downloading the file. (Normally, you can upload to any service free of connect charges.)

I have to dial long distance to log on to a computer information system. Is there anyway I can save money on my phone bills?

Remember, it usually costs less to call anywhere long distance in the evening, on weekends, or during holidays. Call your long distance service for advice about special rates and services. For instance, if you have AT&T's Reach-Out America plan, it's cheaper to dial an out-of-state access number instead of a long distance instate one.

APPENDIX ONE
Common Editing Marks

Use these symbols to make simple corrections on a manuscript. Write the correct information directly above the mistake if it is only one or two words. To add a complete sentence or paragraph, write "Insert Copy A." At the bottom, or on another sheet, write Copy A, with the correct information. If you must insert information in more than one place, label them "Copy B, Copy C, etc." Delete words by drawing the "delete" symbol through the word. For more than one word, draw a line through everything that is to be deleted, and place the delete symbol in the middle.

#	Insert space	⌐H	Start new paragraph
⊙	Add period	⤸	Delete word or phrase
/	Use lower case	*STET*	Disregard the correction
_a_	Use upper case	∧	Insert
⌣	Close up space	∨	Insert
sam︱ple	Transpose		

APPENDIX TWO
Resources

Books for Beginning Writers and Artists

Books for You to Make, Susan Purdy, Lippincott, 1973.

Draw and Write Your Own Picture Book, Mark Thurman and Emily Hearn, Pembroke Press.

How A Book Is Made, Carol Greene, Children's Press, 1988.

Where Do You Get Your Ideas? Sandy Asher, Walker, 1987.

Books for Advanced Pre-Teens and Teens

The Artist's Handbook, Ray Smith, North Light Books.

Artist's Market, Writer's Digest Books, updated annually.

The Children's Picture Book, How To Write It — How To Sell It, Ellen E.M. Roberts, Writer's Digest Books, 1981.

Children's Writer's & Illustrator's Market, Writer's Digest Books, updated annually.

Developing The Creative Edge in Photography, Bert Eifer, Writer's Digest Books, 1984.

Drawing on the Artist Within, Betty Edwards, North Light Books.

Drawing on the Right Side of the Brain, Betty Edwards, North Light Books.

Fine Artist's Guide to Showing & Selling Your Work, Sally Prince Davis, North Light Books.

How To Draw and Sell Cartoons, Ross Thomson and Bill Hewison, North Light Books.

How To Take Good Pictures, Eastman Kodak Company, Ballantine Books, 1981.

Humor and Cartoon Markets, North Light Books, updated annually.

Market Guide for Young Writers, Kathy Henderson, Betterway Publications, updated periodically.

North Light Art Competition Handbook, John M. Angelini, North Light Books.

Photographer's Market, Writer's Digest Books, updated annually.

Photographing Your Artwork, Russell Hart, North Light Books.

Photography for Writers, Lawrence F. Abrams, Entwood Publishing, 1986.

The Writer's Handbook, The Writer, Inc., updated annually.

Writer's Market, Writer's Digest Books, updated annually.

Writing Books for Children, Jane Yolen, The Writer, 1976.

Writing for Children and Teenagers, Lee Wyndham, Writer's Digest Books, 1984.

Writing the Natural Way, Gabriele Lusser Rico, J.P. Tarcher, 1983.

Books for Teachers and Parents

Drawing With Children, Mona Brookes.

Home-Life, Cheri Fuller, Honor Books, 1988.

How to Capture Live Authors and Bring Them to Your Schools, David Melton, Landmark Editions, 1986.

Written & Illustrated by . . ., David Melton, Landmark Editions, 1985.

Magazines for Artists, Photographers, and Writers

The Artist's Magazine, P.O. Box 2120, Harlan, IA, 51593.

Byline, Subscription Department, P.O. Box 130596, Edmond, OK 73140.

Popular Photography, 1633 Broadway, New York, NY 10019.

The Writer, Subscription Department, 120 Boylston Street, Boston, MA 02116.

Writer's Digest, Subscription Department, Box 2123, Harlan, IA 51593.

The Writing Notebook, Creative Word Processing, P.O. Box 1268, Eugene, OR 97440.

Additional Resources

The Children's Writing and Publishing Center, The Learning Company, 6493 Kaiser Drive, Fremont, CA 94555. (800) 852-2255. Excellent, easy-to-use, word processing software for children.

Photographing Your Art, The Tooth Fairy, Ltd., P.O. Box 681, Radford, VA 24141. Booklet explains various procedures involved in photographing artwork in order to submit slides to markets and contests.

Kodak Self-Teaching Guide, Customer Service Pamphlet No. AC-2 available from Kodak (50¢ each), Rochester, NY 14650. Includes many tips for taking better photographs, and avoiding simple mistakes, with space to store sample photographs taken based on specific how-to points. Excellent resource for any age.

Organizations

American Society of Magazine Photographers, Inc., 205 Lexington Avenue, New York, NY 10016. Has a variety of books and pamphlets of interest to illustrators and photographers.

GLOSSARY
Words Artists and Photographers Use

art director. Person usually responsible for the physical appearance and layout of a publication; person who coordinates events for an art contest or gallery. (See also **editor.**)

B & W. Black and white photos or drawings.

bracketing. The process of taking photographs at normal exposure settings as well as taking some that may be slightly over- or underexposed in order to insure getting a good picture.

caption. Written material that describes the subject matter of a photo or illustration. Also called "cutline."

contract. A written agreement specifying which rights an editor is buying and what payment the artist or photographer will receive for his submitted work.

contributor's copies. Free issues of a publication, which you receive instead of, or in addition to, payment.

copy. A term for the contents of a manuscript.

cut. To trim unnecessary parts of a manuscript to make it read better or to fit available space. Copies of artwork or photographs ready for layout may also be cut to fit space or improve the visual effect.

deadline. The last day a contest entry will be accepted or the date on which an editor expects to receive material that he intends to publish.

depth of field. The acceptable zone of a sharp, unblurred image in a photo.

draft. What you call your piece of writing or art while you are creating it.

dummy. A preliminary layout of an entire book, which shows roughly where both text and illustrations will appear.

editor. A person who edits; also a person who among other responsibilities, accepts or rejects manuscripts, artwork, and photographs for publication and has the authority to edit material. For artwork and photos, these duties may be assumed or shared with the art director.

feature. A nonfiction article that usually gives extra background information about a subject and is often accompanied by artwork or photos.

freelance artist, photographer, or writer. A person who works on his own, then selects markets to submit material and ideas to.

illustrations. Photographs or artwork used alone or with a manuscript, which are sometimes supplied by the writer, or arranged for separately with an artist or a photographer.

international reply coupon (IRC). Special coupons, which people can buy at the post office, to include with a self-addressed envelope and are redeemable for local postage for use by markets in countries other than the one the submitter lives in.

layout. A working diagram of a page, with type, illustrations, and margins indicated in the correct position.

lead time. The amount of time needed by a publication to collect and prepare material for use in an upcoming issue.

line art. Illustration in which solid lines are black (usually) and the rest of the art area is white, such as in a basic cartoon.

manuscript. A creative written work prepared on paper.

market. Any publication, contest, or other source that considers material from writers, photographers, or artists with or without the guarantee of payment.

masthead. The section in a newspaper, magazine, or other publication giving the publication's name, the owner's name, and the names of the staff members, including the editor and art director.

mechanical. A piece of heavy paper or board on which the art and text have been pasted, in their final form, to be shot by the printer's camera to make films from which the final publication pages will be printed.

medium. The material you use to create your work, such as crayons, charcoals, acrylic watercolors, etc.

model release form. A paper signed by someone interviewed, photographed, or serving as a model giving permission to the creator to use the material, photo, or artwork for a specific purpose. If the person is a minor, the paper must also be signed by a parent or guardian.

query. A letter asking an editor or art director if he would be interested in seeing a manuscript you have written; an illustrator or photographer may include examples of his work when requesting assignments to supply work to the publication.

rights. What you offer to an editor in exchange for printing your manuscripts, artwork, or photographs.

SASE. An envelope with postage attached (or accompanied by IRC) and addressed to you, which is included in the envelope containing your material or letter when submitting to an editor or other person from whom you would like a response.

signature. A person's name written by himself. In publishing, it refers to a group of pages (usually eight, sixteen, or thirty-two sheets), which are the result once the press sheet has been folded and cut. Most picture books are printed in two sixteen-page signatures.

slide sleeve. A plastic page that holds twenty 35mm slides so that they may all be viewed at once.

solicited material. Work that an editor has asked for or agreed to see before being sent by the creator.

speculation. When an editor agrees in advance to look at your work but there is no guarantee he will accept it for publication or display, the editor says he will look at it "on speculation"; also "on spec." Also refers to the manufacturing instructions for a publication, which indicate what kind of ink and paper will be used, how it will be bound, etc.

tearsheet. A sample of your published work that has been taken (torn) from the publication in which it was printed. Can also be a photocopy of your published work.

"to market." To submit your work to a publication in the hopes of having it accepted for publication.

transparencies. Developed color slides, not color prints.

unsolicited material. Work that is submitted to a publication but an editor did not specifically ask to see.

vanity publisher. A publisher who charges a person the cost of publishing their work, usually a book. Also called a subsidy publisher.

word length. The maximum number of words a manuscript or caption should contain, as determined by the editor or guidelines sheet.

Index